D0951672

KEVIN ADAMS

FINDING YOUR STORY
IN THE PSALMS

SQUARE
INCH

Grand Rapids, Michigan

150: Finding Your Story in the Psalms © 2011 by Square Inch, an imprint of Faith Alive Christian Resources, Grand Rapids, Michigan. All rights reserved. With the exception of brief excerpts for review purposes, no part of this book may be reproduced in any manner whatsoever without written permission from the publisher. For information or questions about the use of copyrighted material in this resource please contact Permissions, Faith Alive Christian Resources, 1700 28th Street SE, Grand Rapids, MI 49508-1407; phone: 1-800-333-8300; fax: 616-726-1164; email: permissions@faithaliveresources.org.

Printed in the United States of America.

We welcome your comments. Call us at 1-800-333-8300 or email us at editors@faithaliveresources.org.

Library of Congress Cataloging-in-Publication Data
Adams, Kevin.
    150: finding your story in the Psalms / Kevin Adams.
       p. cm.
    Includes bibliographical references (p.   ).
    ISBN 978-1-59255-560-4
    1. Bible. O.T. Psalms—Criticism, interpretation, etc.
    I. Title.
    BS1430.52.A33   2011
    223'.206—dc23
                                                        2011023552

10 9 8 7 6 5 4 3

To Gerry Ann:
What shall I return to the L<small>ORD</small> for all his goodness to me?
—Psalm 116:12

To Luke, Rachel, and JJ:
Take delight in the L<small>ORD</small>,
and he will give you the desires of your heart.
—Psalm 37:4

66 Kevin Adams sees the powerful, unrivaled way in which the psalms speak out transformatively, one poem at a time, one person at a time, one crisis at a time, one elation at a time. Readers will find Adams bringing these poems to their lives as well, mediating our pain to God and our hope from God. The book is a gift that keeps on giving . . . as long as the poetry lasts. 99

Walter Brueggemann
Columbia Theological Seminary

66 The highest compliment I can pay to this book is after I finished reading it I was eager to preach on the 99 psalms again."

Haddon Robinson
Harold John Ockenga Professor of Preaching
Gordon-Conwell Theological Seminary

66 The psalms are like the gift of tongues; they are the way the Spirit gives us words when we don't know how to pray. The psalms give us prayer language for elation and lament, praise and doubt, fear and hope. What a gift! This marvelous little book is also a gift, inviting us to see the psalms anew—as an ancient prayer book that speaks poignantly to our postmodern context. Far from some dusty old collection of 'religious' prayers, the psalms are gritty, honest encounters with the living 99 God. A wonderful resource.

James K.A. Smith
professor of philosophy at Calvin College
author of *Desiring the Kingdom* and *Letters to a Young Calvinist*

66 John Donne, Kanye West, Leonard Bernstein, Metallica, Dietrich Bonhoeffer, *Seinfeld,* the God of the psalms— they're all here in their own words. If you can't find yourself in this amazing tour of life, you aren't yet fully human. If C.S. Lewis were a 21st-century California church planter, he would write 99 this book.

Neal Plantinga
author of *Engaging God's World*

CONTENTS

PREFACE

It is one thing to visit a city as a tourist—to see its neighborhoods through a train window, to gaze at its skyline from a nearby hillside, to buy souvenirs from its well-stocked gift shops. It is quite another to engage a beautiful city as a pilgrim—to wander its alleys, to listen to the voices of the people in its shops, to feel its pulse and smell its aromas. For a tourist it's a stop; for a pilgrim it's a destination the heart has longed for.

Often those who read the book of Psalms do so as tourists. Like sightseers, they drop in and look around for an especially pleasing image or a well-known phrase, and then leave, inspired for a time but essentially unchanged. This book invites us to enter the book of Psalms as pilgrims—to linger over these ancient poems, to taste their zesty images, to pay attention to their sharp edges and odd angles that challenge us and promise to transform us. Reading this book, you will find yourself underlining an especially poignant verse here or jotting notes in the margin there, as the psalms come alive through the stories of those who have used and abused them through the centuries.

The book of Psalms is so vast and so intense that our encounter with it can often leave us overwhelmed, like a pilgrim who arrives at a bus station in a new city with a hundred neighborhoods to explore. Like a wise guide who knows the unique corners of the city, Kevin Adams shepherds us to eleven very different psalms and invites us to dwell with them, to absorb their messages, their metaphors, their convictions about God and the world. These eleven psalms then become places that begin to feel like home, preparing us for future explorations that reach into each of the Psalter's many neighborhoods.

One of the main differences between tourists and pilgrims is that pilgrims engage in their journey out of a passion for discovery rather than the hope of an interesting diversion or a nice vacation. Pilgrims travel hard, fully engaged in the moment, expecting that the process will profoundly change them. Ambrose, a fourth-century preacher, once called the psalms a "gymnasium of the soul"—a vast spiritual fitness center. The comparison prevents us from thinking that we should engage the psalms with anything less than deep breaths and flexed muscles, but it also promises exhilaration, the "runner's high" that comes with a surprising discovery or a profound engagement with the God these poems praise and ponder.

In the end, it is not our hard work that breaks open the spiritual blessings of the psalms, but the power of the Spirit who inspired them. These deeply human, emotionally honest cries of praise and pain come ultimately from God's Spirit, not from us. The Spirit who inspired the psalms and providentially guided their compilation now warmly calls us to study them, pray them, and meet God in them. In the biblical psalms, with this book as fitness coach and pilgrimage guide, you will find yourself in that strange and wonderful place where the living God meets face to face with real people at life's raw edges, the very place where the Spirit shapes us in grace and truth.

It is particularly gratifying to commend this book in light of its connections to a Worship Renewal Grant awarded by the Calvin Institute of Christian Worship to Granite Springs Church in 2008 for a program led by Kevin Adams. This grants program is designed to help congregations transform practices of public worship so that they invite worshipers to engage the Christian faith not as tourists but as pilgrims, and that they participate in worship as if they were in a spiritual gymnasium rather than an amusement park or museum. We are especially interested in ways that worship practices can be more deeply connected with the life of a congregation all through the week. As you read this book, you'll encounter not only references to pop culture icons and historical figures but also to a number of poignant moments in the life of Granite Springs Church. Experiences of illumination and grace are altogether possible in very ordinary places. This is a splendid book, one that will open your eyes to the ways God is already at work in your own life and context—and to the ways God will work more deeply in your future.

John Witvliet
Calvin Institute of Christian Worship
Calvin College and Calvin Theological Seminary

INTRODUCTION

A Very Special Grace

"Among all the books the Psalter certainly has a very special grace. . . . within it are represented and portrayed in all their great variety the movements of the human soul. . . . You find depicted in it all the movements of your soul, all its changes, its up and downs, its failures and recoveries."[1]

—Athanasius

"When read only occasionally, these prayers are too overwhelming in design and power and tend to turn us back to more palatable fare. But whoever has begun to pray the Psalter seriously and regularly will soon give a vacation to other little devotional prayers and say: '"Ah, there is not the juice, the strength, the passion, the fire which I find in the Psalter. It tastes too cold and too hard."'"[2]

—Martin Luther

Natan Sharansky refused to leave. Dropping to the ground, he lay on the snowy airport tarmac, insisting he wouldn't budge until his KGB escorts returned his most prized possession. For ten years he had been their prisoner. For more than a year his captors had held him in Moscow's Lefortovo penitentiary, often in the solitary confinement of his special torture cell. Later they upgraded his detention, transferring him to a notorious prison camp in the Siberian gulag. Now he was on his way to freedom. Authorities had given him clean clothes, a long blue overcoat, even a scarf and typical Russian hat. They were trying to lead him away from prison. "You have everything you are permitted to have," they said. But Sharansky was resolute, remaining in the snow.

His wife, Avital, had emigrated to Israel the day after their wedding. The couple had hoped to be together in a few months. It would take twelve years.

Soon after Avital's departure, Soviet officials convicted Sharansky of spying for the United States and sentenced him to thirteen years of hard labor. During his imprisonment Avital relentlessly campaigned for his release. Sharansky spent hundreds of days on hunger strikes and in punishment cells. Finally high-ranking political powerbrokers worked an elaborate international deal on his behalf that included his exchange for Soviet spies captured in the West.

On the verge of freedom, Sharansky stubbornly refused to board the airplane until his captors returned his treasure—a Hebrew book of psalms. It was the only piece of property he took with him to freedom.

Sharansky's act seems beyond belief. Why would anyone risk remaining in a Gulag prison over a book of psalms?

The book was a gift Avital had managed to send with the help of a tourist, just before Natan's arrest. At that time he was neck-deep in his struggle for freedom and dodging agents of the KGB. Every day had new demands. "I had no time for . . . reading psalm books, so I put it aside."

Only when he was locked away in prison, having learned that his father had died and feeling exasperated that he couldn't support his grieving mother, did Sharansky begin reading the book. It was difficult at first. His Hebrew was limited. He couldn't even find the end of a sentence. But slowly he started to understand a word, a phrase. "I remember the first psalm which I suddenly understood, the phrase . . . was 'and when I go through the valley of death, I'll fear no evil, because you are with me.' It was such a powerful feeling, as if King David himself, together with my wife, together with my friends, came to prison to save me from this, and to support me."[3]

That's a feeling Billy Collins could understand too. Collins's poems can make you laugh out loud as though you're at a Saturday night comedy club or reading the Sunday funnies. In 2001, as poet laureate of the United States, Collins worked tirelessly to show ordinary citizens that poetry is not merely an "endangered species in the protected cage of university English departments." He urged teachers to read poems to their high school students without assigning related homework or discussing them into oblivion. It was, he said, a way to help adolescents recover the natural pleasures of poetry after years of having teachers beat it out of them. Collins wanted to bring poetry back into the hearts and minds of ordinary people.

Days after the destruction of the World Trade Center on September 11, 2001, the new poet laureate was asked what role poetry could play in a time of crisis. Collins answered that for him poetry was "a private art and needed a private focus." But in a public radio interview on September 11 itself, Collins "suggested that almost any page of any book of poetry would be 'speaking for life . . . against what happened today.' Or, he said, read the Psalms."[4]

What Collins suggested actually did happen. In the days following 9/11, major media outlets quoted poetry more often than at any other time since the nineteenth century. And the nation heard the psalms.

Sung by Muslims and Jews, by Protestants and Catholics, by Bob Marley and Johann Sebastian Bach, the psalms express the faith of a thousand generations. Every day this ancient prayer book is used by Jewish feminists in New York's Greenwich Village and fourth genera-tion Dakota ranchers driving F-150s. George Herbert, a sixteenth-century British court poet, and Kanye West, a rapper from the gritty streets of Chicago, are just two of the many people who have reworked psalms over the ages to express their deepest hopes and fears. Over the years, psalms have been prayed with equal vigor by a monk chant-ing in a chilly medieval German cloister (Martin Luther), an orphaned teen in Communist Poland (Karl Wojtyla, who would become Pope John Paul II), and a Pakistani pastor in a half-built church who struggles to give his congregation a voice in a culture dominated by Islam.

In an interview, political analyst David Gergen asked Peter Gomes, minister of the Memorial Church at Harvard University, where people who are unfamiliar with the Bible but curious to learn its message should begin reading. Gomes answered without hesitation,

My advice has always been start with an accessible book, and I suggest you start with the psalms. Now people will say, "Oh, but the psalms are so pretty and musical; shouldn't I take something stronger?" If you read the psalms, read them all, and read them at a pretty intense clip—don't spend all year doing it, do it over the course of a couple of weeks—you will find in those 150 psalms such an acute range of human experience you'll think it has been written by your therapist.[5]

In a real sense, psalms *are* simple. They are the "Twinkle, twinkle little star" of biblical teaching, conjuring a child's world of complete trust. Generations of monks have begun their chants with, "O LORD, come to my assistance" (Psalm 70:1). Following Jesus' lead, countless believers have echoed Psalm 31:6 with their dying breath: "Into your hands I commit my spirit." Some psalms, like Psalm 23, offer familiar words of calm during our most troubled times.

But like anything sturdy enough to capture people's deepest feelings for three millennia, the psalms are also complex. They carry the weight of human longing and unspoken creaturely passions. Many overstep our sense of spiritual propriety. Wild with emotion, they voice deep anguish, shout delight, and blubber gut-wrenching personal tragedy. Within a single psalm, Psalm 139, the psalmist beseeches with heartfelt piety, whispers gratitude, offers insightful psychological introspection, bellows a vindictive harangue against enemies, and ends with a touching prayer. Whatever our continent or generation or mood or level of faith, psalms promise to stir and nourish our soul.

This is a book about psalms. But it's also a book about prayer, a certain kind of prayer. Psalms are wonderful and terrible, attractive and repulsive. They are at once familiar and foreign, alien and allies, a comfort and a mystery. We love them and we hate them. Often we frame our prayers with sterile devotion, and our devotion ends without truly expressing our hearts, without gaining audience with the Almighty. Feeling the bankruptcy of our own prayer, we cash in our chips and walk away empty, convinced that faith doesn't work.

Pop artist Jewel, a young woman whose albums have sold millions, expressed this in an interview several years ago with *Rolling Stone*. She said, "I'm just a person who is honestly trying to live my life and asking, 'How do you be spiritual and live in the world without going to a monastery?'"[6]

For generations people have answered that question by praying the psalms. Bridging culture gaps and generational canyons, the psalms connect us with those who long ago experienced our sorrow, suffered our betrayal, bawled our complaint, bore our illness. Capturing our experiences in just the right words and images, the psalms assure us that we are not alone. In the psalms, said C. S. Lewis, "no historical readjustments are . . . required, we are in the world we know."[7]

To help you enter the psalms' special brand of earthy, bone-rattling, candid prayer, this book is filled with stories. Each story is an invitation to see the psalms fresh again— or for the very first time—through the messy and muddled lives of famous and ordinary people, infamous and godly men and women who've loved and prayed them. You're invited to follow their lead and bring these well-tested prayers into your daily experience, to use the psalms as scaffolding for your own life—a trek that promises to be as unsettling as it is comforting.

Hearing the psalms through people's stories, you will find that the family of faith is bigger than you imagine. There's *room*, far more than most of us dream. In the particular faith and doubt, the particular trust and chaos of these particular people, you will find yourself. Faithful or faithless, you'll discover in the psalms words to pray (and whine and murmur) your own questions and convictions. Through these stories you'll find that the psalms are already yours. You'll find that you've already been praying their sort of unique sordid mess—even if you didn't know yet that you were praying. You'll find not only words you long to pray and words you already pray, but a bigger and wider community than you've ever imagined.

Our congregation of both spiritual novices and veterans spent an entire year in the Psalter. Along with inviting people to listen to sermons and study the psalms, we encouraged them to create their own "psalm experiments." One young mom, whose husband was away on a nine-month assignment in the United Arab Emirates, began reading psalms to her young children each evening. The psalms' images so captured them that when they missed a night of reading they insisted on reading two the next night. She also began a second experiment—reading the psalms by herself. "At first they stretched me," she remembers, but soon after starting she wanted to quit. Gradually she found herself struck by the psalmists' honesty. Lacking any sense of restraint, they told God he wasn't "doing his job right." Such honest critique, she said, felt "foreign" and "hard to read" but also "freeing."

Christian monk and scholar Jerome (340-420) so believed in the nourishing power of the psalms that he advised mothers to learn Hebrew and teach it to their children so that they could sing the psalms in the original language. Such advice might appear overzealous to today's overworked parents. But generations later this young California mother understood Jerome's intent. In her crammed daily routine the psalms became prized companions, words that invited her into a larger family she barely knew she had.

With this book I invite you to discover your own story in the honest and earthy world of the psalms. To experience them not through the kind of exegesis that places each Hebrew word under a microscope, but by hearing stories of unlikely prayers and odd pray-ers. The psalms are like an atrium in the house of faith. Their words throw open the corridors of belief, bidding us to bring our faith and doubt inside its community. They encourage us to get to know a God who might be quite unlike the God we now worship or reject. In the psalms God is wilder, more unpredictable, more passionate than we imagine. "God behaves in the psalms in ways he is not allowed to behave in systematic theology," said Benedictine Sebastian Moore. And so do his followers.

OLD FAITHFUL

PSALM 23

"I have read many intelligent and good books in my life. But I did not find anything in them that would have made my heart so quiet and glad, like the four words from that 23rd Psalm "you are with me."[1]

—Immanuel Kant

The Lord is my shepherd; I shall not want.

He maketh me to lie down in green pastures: he leadeth me beside the still waters.

He restoreth my soul: he leadeth me in the paths of righteousness for his name's sake.

Yea, though I walk through the valley of the shadow of death, I will fear no evil: for thou art with me; thy rod and thy staff they comfort me.

Thou preparest a table before me in the presence of mine enemies: thou anointest my head with oil; my cup runneth over.

Surely goodness and mercy shall follow me all the days of my life: and I will dwell in the house of the LORD forever.

—Psalm 23, King James Version

From the outside, life in our fast-growing suburb looks easy. New homes dot rolling hills; excellent schools prepare students for good colleges; ample parks provide soccer moms and dads and their offspring with the latest in designer playground equipment. It's a place of low crime and high economic opportunity—not a place you'd expect to hear a psalm.

But one beautiful April day six hundred people overflowed our church. Most were high school students dressed in black, a stark departure from their typical array of message-bearing T-shirts, spaghetti strap tops, and flip-flops. Many looked lost, like startled deer on a mall parking lot. Church in general, and grief in particular—especially grief for a peer—felt foreign in a way French class never did. Jesse had been a high school junior, one of them. He'd played football and basketball with some, studied math with others, and skipped class with a select few to buy Nikes. Many of these kids had known him since grade school.

The football coach paraded in with his players, a few wearing jerseys. Cheerleaders followed. The state runner-up basketball team, conspicuous by their height, shuffled into a middle row. Jesse's girlfriend, amazingly composed, sat near the front surrounded by family. The building was bursting with adolescents, some leaning against the sanctuary walls. Latecomers watched from an overflow room.

What do you say to high school juniors who have no language for grief? How do you speak to suburbanites enduring their first case of spiritual vertigo, a spinning and disorienting sense that life doesn't always follow their well-managed plans? Where do you find comfort for the grandparents who'd raised Jesse?

Jesse had battled cancer heroically for three years. He'd been baptized in this building only three weeks earlier. Silence fell as his casket was wheeled to the front. This was no moment for religious virtuosos. Nor was it time for a hip band to blast an epic praise song. Time-tested hymns like "Amazing Grace" would be as unfamiliar to those teens as great-grandpa's Studebaker. Several of Jesse's friends shared funny stories. A video montage brought tears. The youth pastor who had visited Jesse every day of his last month of life gave a moving eulogy. But our words alone were not enough. So we began with the psalmist's ancient words that will long outlast us: "The LORD is my shepherd . . . ."

Four months after Jesse's funeral, a chic California senior and her husband of forty years made an appointment with me. We had never met before. They told me they were "not religious." They had formerly been members of a Presbyterian church in the Bay Area but just hadn't gotten a new church after they moved to our town seven years ago. Now they needed to ask me a question: Would I perform her memorial service? ("We don't want it to be a *funeral*," they said.) Decades earlier, cancer had attacked the woman's breasts, and now it was invading her bones.

They began this brave conversation by saying they wanted this service to be a gift to their grown children— two beautiful daughters. "I don't want them to have to think about such arrangements when they're grieving," she said. The couple shared memories. Their love still sparkled forty years after their first meeting in a San Francisco pub. But barely beneath the surface of our conversation about music choices (The Beatles' "Hey Jude" and "Time to Say

Goodbye"—in Italian and English), ambiance (California casual), and care for her body (cremation), the sober reality of death was closing in. It might be a week, or maybe a month. Several times our conversation became too painful and tears rolled down their sun-weathered faces. These were gentle tears. They had cried before and they would cry again.

I found myself liking this couple, so full of good humor and obvious love for life and for each other, so determined to turn a memorial into a celebration. They didn't want anything formal or stuffy. I've been a pastor in California for more than eighteen years. Most people in our town don't even come to church for weddings or burials—instead they have a picnic in a park. Almost all of the memorial services I've performed are for people who don't attend church much. Still, I was struck by the lack of spiritual content as we made plans for this woman's service. Recordings would be played. Friends would tell stories. Photos would line the lobby. Why did they want me, a pastor, to conduct the service? So I asked gently, "Is there any Bible passage that has been a favorite of yours over the years?" There was silence. I was about to shift subjects when the woman said, "What's that one about 'green pastures'?"

"Do you mean 'The LORD is my shepherd . . .'?"

"Yes," she said. "That's the one. I've always liked it. Let's include that one."

Once again, ancient words will be spoken. To high school students staggering under their first grief-induced vertigo, to aging friends celebrating a peer who lived through San Francisco's "flower power" days. How many funerals include Psalm 23? Every single one I've led. It's a familiar pattern that's been repeated for hundreds of years.

Late in his life, Gilbert Greene remembered a trip he once took with Abraham Lincoln. At the time, Lincoln was a young lawyer in Springfield, Illinois. Greene was Lincoln's friend employed as a printer. Occasionally he rode into the country with Lincoln to serve as a witness for an oral will. On this occasion a dying woman dictated her will to the gangly lawyer.

After she was done, she told them how relieved she was to join her family members in heaven. She asked Lincoln to read to her from the family Bible. Instead he began to recite from memory the words of Psalm 23, especially emphasizing the words *though I walk through the valley of the shadow of death I will fear no evil, for Thou art with me. Thy rod and Thy staff, they comfort me. . . .*

Greene recalled that Lincoln went on to quote John 14 from memory: *In my father's house are many mansions. . . .* Lincoln finished by reciting several hymns, closing with "Rock of Ages, Cleft for Me." The woman died while they were still together. Riding back that night, Greene told Lincoln how surprised he was to see him function so perfectly as both lawyer and pastor. Lincoln replied, "God and eternity and heaven are very near to me today."[2]

Over time words shift in meaning and emphasis. Teens cast aside the slang of their parents and even of their elder siblings. A fully loaded car is "hot" and then "cool." Something especially good becomes "bad." Then "sick." "Wicked" becomes the ultimate compliment. In a world of ever-changing vocabulary, today's Shakespeare readers are required to learn another version of English. And for most adolescents, singing along with the radio commercials of Grandpa's growing-up days would be a cross-cultural experience.

Few eighteenth-century novels or nineteenth-century sermons use language that is still compelling or meaningful to today's readers. So why does Psalm 23 still work so well? Why does its meaning stretch undiminished across seven continents and three millennia? Augustine chose it as the hymn of martyrs. Oliver Cromwell died with its words on his lips. The Order of the Odd Fellows began using it in their revised initiation ritual in 1880. Black Panther Eldridge Cleaver recited it during a moment of conversion in a Paris hotel room. Central American children hoping to reunite with their mothers working in the United States recite it while riding the "death train" through Mexico toward the United States.

Maybe Psalm 23 crosses generations and continents because its metaphors and images transcend time and place. Despite its ancient Near Eastern origin, and despite the fact that few people actually know a shepherd themselves, the metaphor of God as shepherd is easily understood. It nourishes trust in any context in any language on any continent.

George Herbert was raised as a gentleman in the English court a continent and two millennia away from David's original setting. Herbert's father died when George was only three years old; his mother raised him and his nine siblings as Anglicans. Described as a man of saintly piety, George also had the unmistakable grace of the upper class. When he was barely out of college, he was elected public orator at Cambridge, representing the university at public events. Soon afterward he served two years in Parliament. Later he took holy orders in the Church of England and spent the rest of his life as rector in Bemerton, where he preached, helped rebuild the church building with his own funds, and wrote poetry.

Herbert's poems have been described as agile, precise, and ingenious. They also resound with a deep, unaffected spiritual devotion. His poem "The Twenty-third Psalm" is among the most famous works in the English language. Portraying the psalmist as a seventeenth-century country parson, Herbert sets himself as coauthor with David.

> The God of love my shepherd is,
> And he that doth me feed;
> While he is mine and I am his,
> What can I want or need?
>
> He leads me to the tender grass,
> Where I both feed and rest;
> Then to the streams that gently pass:
> In both I have the best.
>
> Or if I stray, he doth convert
> And bring my mind in frame;
> And all this not for my desert,
> But for his holy name.
>
> Yea, in death's shady black abode
> Well may I walk, not fear;
> For thou art with me, and thy rod
> To guard, thy staff to bear.
>
> Nay, thou dost make me sit and dine,
> Even in my enemies' sight:
> My head with oil, my cup with wine
> runs over day and night.

Surely thy sweet and wondrous love
Shall measure all my days;
And as it never shall remove,
So neither shall my praise.

The psalm works—whether set in a picturesque seventeenth-century English countryside, in the rap-filled streets of urban Chicago, or even in a public school in Lynnfield, Massachusetts, during the fifties and sixties. One man recalls how the official school prayer was intoned with familiar consistency, like the feel of school paste or the smell of floor wax or the sight of a fifth-grade teacher's khaki pants. Every day the same voice crackled over the loudspeaker, leading every pupil in every class in a recitation of the twenty-third psalm. He remembers that his fellow Roman Catholic kids felt insecure at first since the prayer was spoken in the King James Version, a translation not favored in the Catholic mass. But as in the case of recess lines, multiplication tables, and the pledge of allegiance, repetition worked its magic and the psalm became their own.[3]

Anyone who has experienced the comfort of Psalm 23 can understand why a public school might decide to include it as part of the standard curriculum for every child. Educators of that era assumed that each young American citizen would have a need to say something religious at some point in his or her life. This psalm, with its proven ability to comfort a variety of people, was just the thing. It could be read almost anywhere with universal acceptance—at a Democratic or Republican political convention, at a gathering of used-car dealers or ministers, a group of MTV rappers or church-going seniors. Unlike almost any other text, Psalm 23 speaks comfort in a way that transcends highly charged religious or irreligious boundaries. Bible-belt Southerners and East Coast agnostics, Buddhists and Hindus, Catholics and Protestants, and citizens of various religions participating in a Memorial Day parade have affirmed its inclusion. Even among the most cynical or irreligious, it works.

William Holladay offers multiple reasons for why Psalm 23 became a national treasure: It is short, easily memorized, and undemanding. It never mentions sin. It does not advocate joining a particular religious community. And it can be used in public contexts without offending anyone. Thus it is the ideal spiritual text for a pluralistic culture. "The Lord is my shepherd" offers spiritual words anyone can say to any group at any time.[4]

But what if the familiarity and treasured status of Psalm 23 makes us misunderstand it?

In 1965, the dean and organist of Chichester Cathedral in Sussex commissioned composer Leonard Bernstein to compose music for the psalms. Bernstein seized this opportunity to reframe the age-old insights of Psalm 23 with a fresh perspective. Recycling material from early sketches of his famed musical *West Side Story*, Bernstein composed a collection of psalms in three movements. The second begins with Psalm 23. Bernstein insisted that this piece be sung by a boy treble or countertenor, representing David as a young shepherd boy accompanied by harp. The ancient Hebrew psalmist, remade as a tenor soloist, begins slowly and sweetly. Eventually an angelic choir accompanies him. But then warlike sounds interrupt. Low, rumbling male voices and instruments bellow Psalm 2, "Why do the nations rage?" The harsh disturbance is eventually overpowered by sweet sopranos singing Psalm 23. But the movement's final measures recall the violent interruption, as if to symbolize the unending tangle of conflict and faith.

Bernstein's "Chichester Psalms" reminds us how unwise it is to mindlessly pop Psalm 23 into our lives as a kind of religious pabulum or as a way to avoid painful truth and real threats.

In the movie *Titanic*, Leonardo DiCaprio plays Jack Dawson, a man from steerage who saves the beautiful Rose from marriage to her dull, well-heeled fiancée. The love of Jack and Rose transforms their lives and sets them free. But as they discover, freedom on a sinking ship is limited. As the ship rocks toward its watery grave, they dash between panicked shipmates, fighting to attain higher ground. At one point they pass four members of a string quartet who, moments earlier, had been serenading passengers with classical sonatas. Now the musicians are reciting "The LORD is my shepherd . . ." When the foursome gets to the phrase "yea, though I walk through the valley of the shadow of death," Jack shoves past them. Leading his beloved Rose by the hand he calls, "You want to move a little faster through that valley?"

Jack's the classic Hollywood hero. Handsome and bright, brash and cocksure, he has every confidence that he will save his beautiful girl. But maybe he's right. Maybe a ship's sinking is not the moment for offering sentiment. Maybe it's more a time to put on a life preserver. Could it be that the practical, cynical Jack was acting more in the spirit of the psalms than the psalm-quoting quartet?

At the beginning of Clint Eastwood's 1985 Western, *Pale Rider*, a scoundrel bullies an undersized town of prospectors and their families. Determined to use their land for a hydraulic strip mine, the ruffian schemes to push law-abiding citizens to desert their claims. He sends thugs to pull down their tents and cabins. He transforms the miners' good and simple life into one filled with misery. In an early scene, his bullies have killed the much-loved dog of a settler's young daughter. She kneels, patting the fresh grave. Using the psalm's well-worn words, she has a brand-new dialogue with God:

The LORD is my shepherd; I shall not want. . . .	*But I **do** want.*
He leadeth me beside the still waters;	
He restoreth my soul. . . .	*But they killed my dog.*
Yea, though I walk through the valley of the shadow of death, I will fear no evil:	*But I **am** afraid.*
for thou art with me; thy rod and thy staff they comfort me. . . .	*But we need a **miracle**.*
Surely goodness and mercy shall follow me all the days of my life:	*If you exist.*
and I will dwell in the house of the LORD forever.	*But I'd like to get more of **this** life first.*

Like Bernstein's "Chichester Psalms," this prayer dialogue enables us to view Psalm 23 apart from its frequently over-sentimental overlay. But as Karl Jacobson points out, the miner's daughter prays only part of the psalm. On first viewing, the missing lines—parts of verses 2 and 3 and all of 5—do not seem crucial. But without these phrases the psalm's originally repeated emphasis on God's good care shrivels. Its central claim, "for thou art with me," is challenged. The psalm's familiar words of confidence and trust ring hollow as this little girl faces the reality of death.

To those of us enamored with overly romantic readings of Psalm 23, *Pale Rider* offers a gift. It pushes us from sentimental piety to frank dialogue. The psalm offers time-tested comfort. But why *do* bullies often win? Why *do* seventeen-year-olds die of cancer? Why *do* children grow up amid chaos and poverty? *Pale Rider* helps us see the wisdom of the ancient Hebrew editors who placed this familiar psalm immediately after the heartfelt lament of Psalm 22: "My God, my God, why . . . ?"

And consider "Jesus Walks," Kanye West's rap rendition of Psalm 23. West certainly isn't one to gloss over pain or dodge a frank conversation about injustice. Reset in urban Chicago ("Chi"), these ancient words burn with pain and hope.

> You know what the Midwest is? Young & restless
> Where restless (N*****) might snatch your necklace
> And next these (N*****) might jack your Lexus
> Somebody tell these (N*****) who Kanye West is
> I walk through the valley of the Chi where death is
> Top floor the view alone will leave you breathless
>   Uhhhh!

Try to catch it Uhhhh! It's kinda hard
Getting choked by the detectives yeah yeah now
    check the method
They be asking us questions, harass and arrest us
Saying "we eat pieces of s*** like you for breakfast"
Huh? Y'all eat pieces of s***? What's the basis?
We ain't going nowhere but got suits and cases
A trunk full of coke rental car from Avis
My momma used to say only Jesus can save us
Well momma I know I act a fool
But I'll be gone 'til November I got packs to move
    I hope (Jesus walks)
God show me the way because the Devil trying to
    break me down
(Jesus walks with me)
    The only thing that I pray is that my feet don't
    fail me now
(Jesus walks)
    And I don't think there is nothing I can do now
    to right my wrongs
(Jesus walks with me)
    I want to talk to God but I'm afraid because we
    ain't spoke in so long⁵

Karl Jacobson points out that West, in the tradition
of many poets before him, rewrites the psalm, adjusting
the ancient words to name his own urban reality. David's
"Though I walk through the valley of the shadow of
death" becomes "As I walk through the valley of the Chi
[Chicago] where death is." In West's retelling the "valley of
the shadow of death" is not some distant symbol set in an
ancient Palestinian meadow. The valley is Chicago, a real

place with real problems amid the real struggles of life and death. West prays for Jesus—the shepherd of the psalm—to walk with him in the midst of those struggles.[6]

Like Leonard Bernstein, Jack Dawson, and the miner's daughter in *Pale Rider*, West resets this favorite psalm amid glaring pain, in his case the raw cry of a hurting city center in the twenty-first century. By doing so, he accents the psalm's purpose, calling vulnerable people beyond pious platitudes to something deeper and more desperate—to unvarnished trust. Setting out our desperate need, West echoes the psalm's ancient invitation to trust.

We can't forget that this psalm (and the whole Hebrew Bible in which it is located) is a gift to the world from the Jews. According to Rabbi Margaret Moers Wenig, Psalm 23 is the ideal Sabbath psalm. In some strict homes it is recited five times each Sabbath:

- on Friday night before the conclusion of the service that begins Sabbath
- at dinner that same evening before Kiddush (a blessing over wine that helps "keep" the Sabbath)
- the next day at lunch before Kiddush
- during *Seudat Shelishit* (a late afternoon meal on the Sabbath)
- as part of the meal immediately after Sabbath concludes[7]

For practicing Jews, the trusting rest of the Sabbath is an art form. Rabbi Abraham Heschel writes that the Sabbath is God's good gift designed to restore the human soul. Each Sabbath is an invitation for the community to participate in eternity. In keeping it well believers taste the comfort God will one day bring forever. "On Sabbath we cease from our striving and scurrying and remember we are creation, not creator," says Heschel. "Six days a week we wrestle with the world, wringing profit from the earth; on the Sabbath we especially care for the seed of eternity planted in the soul. The world has our hands, but our soul belongs to Someone Else."[8]

Ancient rabbis, like the Psalter's original editors, often highlighted the value of obeying Torah. But they also warned that excessive piety might actually prevent devoted believers from fulfilling Torah. So they accented the gift of Sabbath rest, highlighting our need to trust in the God who provides, the One who gives life. In the language of Psalm 23, Sabbath is the day God leads us to still waters. It is the day he invites us to his banqueting table. It is the day he restores our soul. As Heschel says, it is the day believers remember they were not first created to work or to repair the world but to enjoy God. God's people are not sweatshop slaves but creatures who bear God's image. How appropriate then, for us to sing this trusting love song each Sabbath.[9]

Seminary professor Rodney Cooper describes the way this theme of trust powerfully shapes African American preaching. He tells the story of a young black preacher and an old black preacher sitting near the pulpit side by side one Sunday morning. The young preacher stood up, walked to the pulpit, and read Psalm 23. The congregation politely said amen. Then the old preacher stood up. He followed the young preacher to the pulpit and read Psalm 23 again. The congregation wept, clapped, and shouted a hearty amen. When the old preacher sat down again, the young preacher asked him why they responded with such emotion to his reading of the psalm. The old man answered, "Son, you read Psalm 23, but I *read* Psalm 23. You can read it, but I have lived it."

African American preachers, Cooper says, "speak prophetically to people whose daily experiences overtly or subtly produce striving and stress due just to being who they are—Black." Black preachers, he explains, must be in touch with the people's pain. Because the first African American preachers were slaves themselves, they preached effectively to their people without formal training. They spoke to issues from their own identity. Today's African American parishioners, he says, often say that Sunday is the only time when they can openly embrace their pain and encourage their hearts, to "let go and let God." So black preaching must continually connect the biblical text to the situation people face today.[10]

Whether sung by Hasidic Jews learning to trust each Sabbath, or by slaves resting from oppressive labor, or by a nineteenth-century Springfield family learning trust in the face of a mother's sudden death, the words of Psalm 23 work. Maybe because intuitively even the most hardened skeptic believes—or wants to believe—in the shepherding heart of God. A drug dealer in Chicago, a Jewish believer in Bosnia, and a high school junior in California want to believe in God's gentle care for people who are lost and weak. Maybe it works because at the center of the story of any one of us is the story of *all* of us. We have the same dreads and dreams and doubts and fears in the night. We spend most of our energy holding ourselves together, but there are moments when we are painfully aware that the job is too big for us . . . and we need to trust someone else.

At twenty, flying was Paul's obsession, his great love. It was also a family tradition. One day he checked out a sturdy twin-prop Cessna from Tulip City Airport so he and a friend could fly north along the west coast of Lake Michigan. Chatting playfully they soared over spectacular sandy shorelines and pristine forests, logging hours to get his full pilot's license. He was to return at midnight.

At first his tardiness made his parents angry. What parent sleeps soundly before his or her child is home safe? By one o'clock they were saying, "Paul, stop doing things like this. Get it home." At two o'clock they called the family to say Paul hadn't come back yet. At four o'clock, voice trembling, they notified their pastor. "Tim, something has gone wrong. Paul's plane hasn't returned." The pastor threw on his jeans and hustled to the airport. At five o'clock family members and close friends huddled together, barely able to sit still on terminal chairs. Waiting.

The clock moved with painful slowness through the morning. Worry spread and deepened like a bad infection. At noon officials from the FAA drove into the airport parking lot. Paul's dad and mom, Dennis and Sally, sprinted out the door. Twenty years later those gathered can still see Sally collapsing in the parking lot. Officials had found Paul's plane in twenty feet of water off the Ludington coast. Their boy was dead.

Amid searing pain, Dennis and Sally staggered back into the terminal. Loved ones circled around them. Tears spilled on each other, hearts opened in grief. Emotions exploded. Dennis pounded his fist on the wall. Parents do all kinds of things when they lose a child. And then, after all their heat, sweat, and pain, Dennis turned to his pastor. "Tim, you've got to pray for us."

No seminary training can prepare a person for such a moment. What on earth do you pray? Who dares mouth pious clichés to a mother and father who have just lost a son? Tim grabbed Dennis under his right arm and a family friend under his left. Sally was held up by friends across the circle as they joined arms together. In that vulnerable moment, Tim reached across the centuries to borrow the words to pray, not trusting his own eloquence or verbal skill. Walking in the footsteps of pastors like Augustine and Ambrose, he prayed, "The LORD is my shepherd, I shall not want. He makes me lie down in green pastures . . ." At that point he broke down and cried. He couldn't pray another word.

A stunning thing happened then. Dennis, whose heart had just been wrenched from his chest, picked up the prayer where Tim left off. "He leads me besides the still waters. . . ." Still waters? Only a few hours ago the angry waters of Lake Michigan had swallowed his boy's plane as it sank to the bottom. Dennis broke down and cried like a baby. Then his wife, Sally, picked up the prayer. Full of grief, she continued ". . . he restores my soul. He guides me in paths of righteousness for his name's sake. Even though I walk through the valley of the shadow of death, I will fear no evil, for you are with me. Your rod and staff will comfort me." She made it as far as the next line: "You prepare a table before me in the presence of my enemies . . ." and then she couldn't go on. What was she thinking about? A thousand peanut-butter-and-jelly sandwiches? Paul's favorite backyard barbeque? A wedding feast that would never happen? She fell, weeping. Her friends tried to hold her up but the pain was too heavy to stand.

Then the most remarkable thing of all happened. Every person in that circle of grief continued praying Psalm 23. With one communal voice they continued the ancient words "You anoint my head with oil, my cup overflows" until they came to final line: "Surely goodness and mercy will follow me all the days of my life, and I shall dwell in the house of the LORD forever."[11]

In the face of immediate and overwhelming pain they joined the ancient, never-ending chorus; they uttered words of trust tested for centuries. They had said these ancient words before—maybe mechanically, without even thinking about them. But this time they were desperate to say them again. In danger of falling apart, they turned to Psalm 23. And, like steel girders holding a bridge upright through a violent hurricane, these words held them fast, assuring them that even in the valley of the shadow of death, fear would not have the last word. At the very moment their emotions spun in violent chaos, those familiar and trusting words held them together. "The Lord is my shepherd. . . ."

DRAGON SLAYERS

Praying in a World of Enemies

PSALM 3

"Here one saw a feeling we all know only too well, Resentment, expressing itself with perfect freedom, without disguise, without self-consciousness, without shame—as few but children would express it today."[1]

—C. S. Lewis

Arise, LORD!
Deliver me, my God!
Strike all my enemies on the jaw;
break the teeth of the wicked.
From the LORD comes deliverance.
May your blessing be on your people.

—Psalm 3:7-8

The rectory was on fire. According to the rector, Samuel Wesley, it was no accident—disgruntled parishioners had ignited it to send their pastor and his family a fiery, unforgettable message. And this wasn't the first time.

Wakened by sparks falling from the thatch roof, Samuel's daughter Hetty fled down the hall to rouse her mother, while Samuel ran through the smoke, gathered his other seven children and the servants, and scuttled them down the stairs. Finding the main hall and front door ablaze, they rushed to escape through the back entrance and windows. His wife, Susanna, was too pregnant to follow. After saying a prayer, she walked naked out through the fiery front door.

Gathered in the garden with the neighbors, the family heard a cry from upstairs. No one had come for five-year-old John. He was still in the attic, trapped by the flames. Samuel ran back and tried to fight his way up the stairs, but the burning floorboards wouldn't hold his weight. Desperately the family knelt in prayer to commend John's soul to the Lord. As they prayed John's face appeared in the window. Leaning across the sill, he screamed for help. There was no time to fetch a ladder, but one neighbor quickly climbed onto the shoulders of another. Wobbling toward the window they snatched him from the wreckage just as the parsonage roof collapsed inward. Once again Samuel knelt in prayer, this time a prayer of thanksgiving for the safe deliverance of his entire family from the flames.[2]

What kind of pastor has parishioners who are willing to commit arson on their own property in order to send him a message? A man with enemies.

Both Samuel and his wife, Susanna, were raised in homes threatened by adversaries. Their fathers were Puritan ministers, steadfast supporters of Cromwell's radically reformed Church of England. When King Charles II displaced Cromwell in 1660 and returned to the throne, dissenting leaders like Samuel and Susanna's fathers were expelled from the state church and became targets of brutal oppression. No doubt the foes Susanna and Samuel faced felt all too familiar, since their own fathers had suffered similar harassment. But even in such troubled times, Samuel seemed especially adept at raising enemies among his parishioners. Sternly inflexible and prone to mismanagement, he routinely alienated his flock. They responded by creating mayhem, repeatedly setting fire to his home. And once they had him arrested at the church for a debt of thirty pounds.

That near-death experience in the burning rectory forever changed John Wesley's life. It shaped the way he thought about himself and his life's mission. As a young man following his father into the ministry, the image of his dramatic, fiery rescue shaped his preaching; he often described himself as "a branch plucked from the fire," a phrase borrowed from the prophet Amos.

Like his parents and grandparents, John Wesley's life was saturated in the psalms. Home-schooled by his mother, the first words young John learned to speak were the Lord's Prayer and portions of the psalms. Soon he was memorizing sections of the Bible, even whole books by heart. As a student at Oxford University, John began a "Holy Club" with friends. Each morning the group met for three hours of morning prayer, reading psalms and the Greek New Testament. Though the Anglican Church required the sacrament of communion only three times a year, the group celebrated communion every Sunday. Following the custom of the ancient church, they fasted on Wednesdays and Fridays.

Sensing an overpowering call to missions, John sailed to North America to serve the emerging colony of Georgia. During the voyage, a raging storm attacked their ship. Angry waves swept over the bow and water poured into the decks below. The mast split into pieces. It was as if the great deep had grabbed the ship with watery arms and was about to plunge its passengers to a watery grave. As the ship thrashed about, his fellow passengers screamed their fright and panic.

But a group of Moravian believers were also aboard that quivering vessel. Known for their sturdy faith and resolute living, these German believers were singing a psalm when the storm began. As the storm roared, they calmly continued to sing. Later on, taken by their trust in that most desperate hour, Wesley asked, "Were you not afraid?" No, they replied; their faith, powered by the psalms, held them strong.

Despite his immersion in the Bible and consistent exposure to the psalms, John, like his father and grandfathers before him, managed to make enemies at every turn. Returning to England after his unsuccessful attempt at mission work in America, a spiritually renewed Wesley preached his evangelical gospel at every opportunity. He could gather a crowd of hundreds simply by walking into a city street and singing a psalm. Church of England traditionalists came to watch him preach—but also to attack him. Encouraged by local clergy or magistrates, mobs frequently disrupted him and his followers, who came to be called Methodists. Methodist buildings were ransacked. Methodist preachers were harassed and beaten.

A favorite tactic of Methodist-baiters was to drive oxen into congregations assembled outdoors for field preaching. Opponents once paid two singers to interrupt John's preaching by performing a ballad during the middle of the worship he was leading. When reasoning with this disruptive duet failed, he instructed the congregation to begin singing a psalm together, and so silenced the provocative guests.[3]

One evening in Wednesbury, a mob attacked the house where Wesley was staying, demanding, "Bring out the minister." Wesley welcomed the ringleaders into the home and quickly made peace with them. Then, standing atop a chair, he addressed the mob. After hearing his message, many swore him allegiance, but enough rabble-rousers remained to drag him off to the justice of the peace, who was asleep in bed. They managed to rouse one of his sons, who asked the mob to describe the nature of their complaint: "Why, an't please you," they answered, "they sing psalms all day; nay, and make folks rise at five in the morning. And what would your Worship advise us to do?" "To go home and be quiet," replied the justice's peace-making son.[4]

Facing their antagonists with resolute determination, Wesley and Methodist followers refused to be squelched. Never one to cower from a fight, Wesley was once barred from speaking at the church in Epworth where his father had served for decades. Instead of leaving in defeat, he addressed a large crowd while standing on his father's tombstone.

Although his opponents' vigorous hostility sometimes dissolved when they learned that Wesley was a well-educated Oxford graduate and a member of the gentry, the Establishment itself regarded Wesley as a traitor to his class. Bringing spiritual hope to the masses was considered dangerous in an age when literacy was restricted to the elite. Conventional church leaders were aghast and frightened by the emotionalism routinely stirred up by Wesley's preaching. Here's how Wesley himself described the response of his listeners at one of his stops: "Many of those that heard began to call upon God with strong cries and tears. Some sank down, and there remained no strength in them; others exceedingly trembled and quaked; some were torn with a kind of convulsive motion. I have seen many hysterical and epileptic fits; but none of them were like this."[5]

Like the Wesleys, most of us have opponents. But in sharp contrast to them, most of us try to steer clear of conflict. If we pray at all, we aim for the kind of prayer that might lower our blood pressure and raise our general level of happiness. We prefer our prayer to serve as a mute button that disables the noisy conflicts of life, leaving us in a peaceful state of unbreakable inner tranquility.

In a well-known episode of *Seinfeld*, Frank receives a "relaxation cassette" from his physician. Whenever he feels his blood pressure rise, he's supposed to say, "Serenity now." The episode opens with Frank in the back seat of his son George's car. In a vintage harangue, Frank orders his wife Estelle to slide her seat forward so he can have more leg room. When Estelle seems unable or unwilling to cooperate, Frank shouts, "Serenity now!" His new exclamation surprises both family members, and they ask where it came from. Frank tells them about the doctor's orders, and George asks, "Are you supposed to yell it?" Frank responds, "The man wasn't specific." Throughout the episode, he repeats his mantra: when Estelle nags him to fix the front door, while stirring a computer sales combat between George and another employee, while Kramer battles neighborhood boys who fling AA eggs at him. Over and over Frank repeats his shouted prayer as a high-decibel mantra: "Serenity now!"

That's often the kind prayer we think we need: a magic pill, easy and effective, to calm our frazzled nerves. It's like self-prescribed medicine. Theologian Eugene Peterson calls it "pseudo prayer." Promising a taste of heaven, offering entry into the subliminal harmony of the universe, it puts us in tune with the general hum of a higher plane. Prayer, we suppose, ought to decrease our stress and ensure a long and peace-filled life. Masters of such prayer present themselves as perpetually calm, unflappable, tranquil in every circumstance.

Psalm prayer, on the other hand, requires us to face life the way it really is. Often, says Peterson, such honest appraisal informs us that things are pretty bad. To our shock we realize that not everyone likes us. We put peace signs on our cars, eat organic food, mow the neighbor's lawn, maybe even attend church, but we still have enemies. And no self-help book or moral advance seems to make them go away. According to the psalms, facing enemies is the typical experience of every believer of every generation and every continent. In prayer we grapple and fight, tackle and wrestle. We battle foes.

Prayer may bring harmony, but only after a face-off with the enemy. Prayer may induce tranquility, but only after we joust with our inner demons. Serenity may emerge, but only by way of Gethsemane and the cross. People craving a calm, hypnotic spirituality find the psalms alarmingly honest. As Peterson writes, in the psalms God is the "primary subject . . . but enemies are established in solid second place." He adds, "When we take the psalms as our guide, we find that people who pray have a lot of enemies, and that they spend a lot of their praying time dealing with them."[6]

C. S. Lewis makes the same observation. The first eleven verses of Psalm 143 are poignant poetry, he writes, bringing tears to our eye. But the poet adds a final verse, almost as an afterthought: "and of thy goodness slay mine enemies" (KJV). Where did that come from? Psalm 139, Lewis notices, has a similarly stunning and unlikely addition. An amazing prayer of self-reflection and introspection, it begins "You have searched me, LORD . . ." That tone lasts until verse 19, when the psalmist suddenly snarls, "Wilt thou not slay the wicked, O God?" (KJV), "as if it were surprising that such a simple remedy for human ills had not occurred to the Almighty."[7]

Enemies slither into even the best-loved psalms. Psalm 8 begins on a high note of wonder and celebration, "LORD, our Lord, how majestic is your name in all the earth!" but in the next line the psalmist adds, "Through the praise of children and infants you have established a stronghold against your enemies. . . ."

People raised with the psalms scarcely notice enemies crouching in their beloved book, mostly because they tend to skip over the pesky ones. But a closer look shows that these enemies are recurring company. One moment you're in a tranquil green pasture praying "The LORD is my shepherd"; the next you're shocked to hear yourself pray, "You prepare a table before me in the presence of my enemies."

It is, says Lewis, as if "the poet's enjoyment of his present prosperity would not be complete unless those horrid Joneses (who used to look down their noses at him) were watching it all and hating it."[8]

Of her childhood, Janet McCann says, "We were not a Bible family." The family attended a Presbyterian church "on Easter, Christmas, and other times when someone thought about it." Most Sunday mornings, she writes, her family read comics like *Blondie*, not the Bible. Then, while she was in grade school, her maternal grandfather became sick. Because Janet was too young to be allowed to visit, her mother drove her by so she could wave to a stick figure her mother said was her grandfather. During the upheaval of his illness, Janet's family enrolled her in a local Bible school where, for each psalm Janet memorized, she received a bird sticker. Soon, she says, she had a whole aviary.[9]

Decades later, the psalms still speak to Janet in ways both beautiful and frightening. Beautiful because they provide landscapes of solace and green valleys, places of running water, olives, and flourishing figs. And frightening "because of how warlike they are, how much they seem to be asking God for military support." Rereading the psalms now as an accomplished poet, McCann says, "I feel very tiny . . . menaced on all sides by creatures out of my grandson's imaginations: My Enemies." There are only three presences in the psalms: the speaker, God, and the Enemy, "who moves in the margin like a dragon on the edge of the map."[10] These enemies appear in most psalms: as a ferocious beast, a mocking betrayer, a vicious dog, a sword-wielding terrorist, a well-trained soldier, a well-published slanderer. Each, in McCann's imagination, is a sort of dragon.

———————————

Nancy Price's novel *Sleeping with the Enemy* became a movie starring Julia Roberts and Patrick Bergin. Presumably, heroine Laura Burney has everything any woman could ever want: a luxurious ocean-front home, a handsome investment counselor husband, all the possessions money can buy. But Laura's marriage, like so many marriages, is not what it seems. When her husband, Martin, interprets her playful bantering with a neighbor as flirting, he strikes her face and then kicks her as she lies on the ground, weeping. As the movie continues, we learn that his abuse had begun soon after their wedding day. To escape from her husband, she fakes her own drowning and runs away from her enemy to the safety of a small town in Iowa. But like enemies in the psalms and in real life, her husband follows like a predator stalking his elusive prey.

As a pastor I hear many stories about people who are "sleeping with the enemy." A little girl's father says in a tone she will never doubt, "You'll never amount to anything." She carries his condemnation with her into her eighties. A father watches helplessly as his teenage son acts out his violent depression by smashing a whole watermelon against the living room ceiling. A wife watches in shock as her military-trained husband flings knives around the house. A teenage daughter screams at her mother, "No wonder you're still single, you're such a bitch." A husband learns that his wife is having an affair with their teenage neighbor. A gay son tells his father about his sexual orientation, only to hear the father say he never wants to see him again.

A friend told me that after her husband returned home from a months-long work assignment, he informed her that he was leaving her and moving in with another woman. Crushed, but determined to move on with her life, she posted the serenity prayer[II] in every room in her house: "Grant me the serenity to accept the things I cannot change, the courage to change the things I can, and the wisdom to know the difference." That prayer, almost as well-loved and well-used as the Lord's Prayer or any psalm, makes sense to me. But I wonder if my friend would be wiser to also post psalms throughout her home that might help her fearlessly face the dragons that have overturned her seemingly settled life.

What married person doesn't occasionally (or regularly) look at the person in the other side of the bed and wonder, "How did I marry *you*?" A few years ago I attended a marriage conference. I would like to say I attended it because I'm a wise and thoughtful husband dedicated to maximizing my matrimonial skills and becoming the stellar partner my wife deserves. The truth is that I was dragged there, feeling sullen and aggrieved. Arms crossed, seated in the back row, I was determined to remain uninvolved, defying the upbeat speakers to change my mood. Seated in that hotel ballroom with hundreds of other couples I wondered resentfully, *What could these hotshot speakers* (preachers, many of them!) *teach us, twelve years into our marriage?* One of the first group exercises—and the idea of participating in group exercises was one of the many reasons I desperately did not want to be there—was to hold hands with your spouse, look deep into his or her eyes, and say, "You are not the enemy." Fifteen years later that is the most helpful thing my wife and I remember from the conference. It's an exercise we occasionally repeat.

At one time or another, most of us sleep with an enemy, or at least we harbor one under our own roof. Denise Hopkins reports that some elderly parents hear in the psalms' enemy language a description of their adult children. They suspect their offspring of vigilantly searching for the first signs of senility in their parents. One wrote, "They're just waiting for me to leave the stove on when I go out or forget my keys one more time, then, one, two, three, I'll be put in the nursing home." In the same way, hospital patients frequently view their own physicians as enemies. How could anyone with their best interest in mind prescribe another needle jab, an invasive test, or a treatment that makes them feel sick?[12]

Employees view supervisors with suspicion and peers as competitors, especially in a slack economy. And anyone who has attended junior high school knows the particular dragons of education: math problems assigned by teachers purely as a form of torture, peers who swear their allegiance one moment only to betray you the next, vice-principals who are always watching for the slightest misstep, parents who force you to attend such a wretched place in the first place.

If only we could run to church to find refuge, a safe, nurturing community of faith. But enemies even manage to insinuate their way into churches. A few years ago, a survey showed that the average pastor leaves church because of three people. Three people, it seems, are enough to make a pastor's life unbearable. But every pastor knows that survey is wrong. It only takes one.

———————

Even spiritual giants face enemies. Moses' own sister and brother turned against him. The prophet Jeremiah's royal enemies tossed him into a pit. The apostle Paul endured beating and ridicule with surprising grace, but fought off any who might plunder or weaken the tender new churches he began. One wonders if Paul had Psalm 3 in mind when he became so fed up with troubling parishioners that he fumed, "Warn a divisive person once, and then warn them a second time. After that, have nothing to do with them" (Titus 3:10). In a fascinating letter to Christians living in the Vegas-like atmosphere of the ancient Greek city of Corinth, Paul wrote his poignant, eloquent poem about love—"Love is patient, love is kind . . ." (1 Corinthians 13). In another chapter of this same letter, apparently seeing no contradiction, he suggested that one outrageously disobedient member be "handed over to Satan" so his "spirit [could] be saved on the day of the Lord" (5:5).

Jesus sparred with Bible-thumping Pharisees, politically savvy Roman authorities, and even his own family, who on one occasion came to "collect" him, fearing he was out of his mind. It was hyper-religious people who turned out to be his worst enemies. In one of the best surprises of the Bible, Jesus never treated spiritual novices or honest skeptics as enemies; they became his most loyal friends and ardent followers.

For Moses and Paul and Jesus and us, enemies are simply there—in the best lives and schools and neighborhoods and prayers. They vex and haunt, taunt and ridicule, mock and betray, knife our reputation and slander our good name. They ruin God's creation, and, according to Eugene Peterson, they ruin God's good intentions for us. That's why the enemies in the psalms are not just the enemies of a particular person; they are God's enemies as well.

Psalm 3 is the first "real" prayer in the Psalter. Following the Psalter's two-part introduction (Psalms 1 and 2), in which the psalmist pledges lifelong love and study of the Torah, the psalmist here addresses God directly: "Lord, how many are my foes . . ." Faced with enemies, like most of us, he prays for help.

In Psalm 3, that request for help is very specific.[13] The psalm's heading reads: "A psalm of David. When he fled from his son Absalom." Absalom, David's favorite son, has ignited a coup. His well-laid plans launch a civil war designed to remove David and elevate Absalom to the throne. David, the elderly and embarrassed father, flees for his life. All sorts of scoundrels join the fray, spraying him with dirt and pelting him with stones and insults. The story is frighteningly familiar. Isn't that how our life goes? We're simply doing our job, paying our bills, raising our children, coaching a sports team, and suddenly we're dealing with an enemy.

For fifteen years I moonlighted as a soccer coach. Each new season I dreamed of transforming average suburban athletic cast-offs into candidates for World Cup glory. I coached four-year-olds and adolescents, novices and veterans, the coordinated and the clumsy. Most players and parents became friends. Each Saturday we gathered to compete against common foes, facing rival parents and players whose very presence across the soccer field bonded us into one unified team. Together we battled elbowing opponents, harsh weather, and sometimes incompetent refs. But during my decade and a half of coaching, there were a few times when a player or parent on our own team became my foe.

One dad was particularly peeved at my standard beginning-of-the-year speech. Each year we established guidelines for in-game etiquette: "Parents, please let the coach instruct your children during the game so the players will hear one unified message and not fifteen varying ones." First this soccer dad defied our team ethos by ordering his son to visit him for half-time instruction in full view of teammates and fellow parents. Rather than huddle with his team and coach, this player strategized with his father.

When the wise and gentle coach reminded this rogue parent of the mutually-agreed-upon team etiquette, the soccer dad shifted his strategy and geography. He avoided greeting—or even seeing—the coach and his fellow parents. Before each game he marched to the opposite side of the soccer field and watched the play from his strategically located camp-chair. At half-time his son would dutifully trot across the field to hear his dad's private coaching, eschewing his coach and fellow players.

Enemies, it turns out, not only find us at work and when we're with our families, but also when we're volunteering for community service. Enemies are everywhere. Sleeping in our home, standing beside us at work, sitting across the soccer field—and, thankfully, in the psalms.

The headings attached to some psalms link them with particular stories. Seventy-three are tied to David's story; thirteen of those refer us to exact episodes in his life. All tell a particular story with a particular trouble: "When the LORD delivered him from the hand of all his enemies, and from the hand of Saul" (Psalm 18). "When he feigned madness before Abimelech so that he drove him out and he went away" (Psalm 34). "When he fled from Saul, in a cave" (Psalm 57). "When Saul sent men to watch his house in order to kill him" (Psalm 59) And here in Psalm 3, "When he fled from his son Absalom." David's enemy lives under his own roof, eats at his table, wears clothes he purchased, uses his chariot, and stabs him in the back. Even King David, God's favorite, knows the particular misery of betrayal.

Over the years, astute psalm observers have noted the "strange and bitter irony" that the king once had to flee from Absalom, his own son.[14] Rabbi Shimon bar Yochai, a spiritual leader of the Bar Kochba Revolt against Rome in A.D. 135, and one of the forerunners of the Jewish mystical movement Kabbalah noted the distinct change. In Psalm 2 David belittles the conspiracies of the nations: "Why do the nations conspire and plot in vain . . . The One enthroned in heaven laughs; the Lord scoffs at them" (verses 1, 4). But the threat of his own son's rebellion soon shifts his tone: "LORD, how many are my foes!" (Psalm 3:2). The rabbi concluded, "From here we see that a bad upbringing (that is, a rebellious child) in one's house is worse than the war of Gog and Magog." An unruly child a more troubling foe than the cataclysmic wars of end times?

Rabbi Bahya ibn Paquda, eleventh-century author of *Chovot ha-Levavot* (Duties of the Heart), a classic on Jewish ethics, goes a step further. Referring to Psalm 3 he cautions, "Our enemy lies between our ribs." In this spirit, after ten centuries of use, Talmudic sages found it necessary to add an additional blessing to their *Amidah*, the ancient rhythm that guides daily prayers. As if they'd just read numerous psalms, they titled this extra blessing "The blessing of the heretics." This one and only negative prayer in the liturgy reads, in part, "Blessed are you, Lord God, who breaks down enemies and humbles sinners."

In the monastic tradition, especially in the rule of St. Benedict, Psalm 3 is routinely spoken as the first psalm. Each day begins, "I laid me down and slept, I awakened for the Lord sustained me." Benedict believed that in the simple act of rising we face the tasks of the new day, tasks that so often include facing enemies.

Following those ancient guidelines one morning, four friends and I woke to attend the 3:30 a.m. vigil at a local monastery, joining the eighteen Trappists in residence who sing through the entire Psalter every two weeks. We began with Psalm 70: "O Lord, come to my assistance." Then we launched into ancient early morning chants, starting with Psalm 35: "Contend, O Lord, with those who contend with me. Fight those who fight against me." Following the psalm, we asked God to "draw the spear and javelin" against our pursuers and "let their way be slippery." Next we prayed through Psalm 36: "I have a message from God in my heart concerning the sinfulness of the wicked" who "plot mischief while on their bed." We continued with Psalm 37: "Do not fret because of the wicked or be envious of wrongdoers, for like the grass they will soon wither."

Seated foggy-brained on a wooden pew in the shadows of a beautiful full moon at this predawn vigil, I found myself wondering, what enemies do these cloistered monks battle? They live on 500 acres of fertile vineyards and orchards in a peaceful spot along the meandering Sacramento River. Their ancient vow of poverty makes them unlikely competitors of agribusiness conglomerates and more well-funded California wineries. *Enemies?* In a rural California town of forty-eight people?

Like the ancient rabbis, well-regarded monastic teachers warn students about the enemies within. Certainly we deal with antagonistic enemies, even inside our own community. But such individuals can be less dangerous than our own self-destructive tendencies and unrestrained cravings. Our inner voices often require of us greater vigilance and alertness than external forces. We are, as the saying goes, our own worst enemy. We say something stupid. We hurt a colleague's feelings. We damage an acquaintance's reputation. We betray the confidence of a friend. The first Christian monks didn't move to the desert to escape the world but to battle their inner demons. Like those early Christians, we too regularly battle the untamed dragon of our own heart.

But if we reduce every enemy in the psalms to "the enemy within," we lose a precious prayer resource and connection with reality. Prayer is a form of conflict, a clash between agendas. No wonder people who practice psalm prayer get excited. To pray the psalms well is to name and identify our enemies.

———————————

Eric Sarwar is a Presbyterian pastor who loves the psalms. Check his Facebook status and you'll read lines like "Worked all night at the studio," "Spent the evening sequencing music and the vocals are tremendous," and "Took service at village church." Nothing too unusual about that—except that Eric works in Pakistan, where Christians are a tiny discarded minority, so his Facebook status also includes alarming updates like "Young Christian boy murdered in police custody" and "Police fired shells on rally and arrested Christian protestors."

Sarwar is on a mission. He's determined to help Pakistani Christians reclaim a heritage of singing psalms in Punjabi set to indigenous melodies and rhythms. One hundred years ago missionaries worked hard to establish schools, hospitals, and churches in Pakistan, hoping faith would spread from these helpful organizations. Their stellar efforts, most often using Urdu, the official language, reached mostly educated, city people. I. D. Shahbaz, a local scholar, poet, and Anglican pastor, translated the psalms into the poetic Punjabi language and set them to bhajan folk tunes, repetitious songs with simple call and response lines called *zaboors*. They were an instant hit. Soon preachers could gather bazaar-size throngs merely by singing Punjabi psalms.

The ranks of Punjabi Christians grew quickly. Soon Anglicans, Baptists, Catholics, and other Christians included Punjabi *zaboors* in their hymnals. But as that first generation of Christians died, the psalm tunes faded from collective memory. In their place, Sarwar says, believers began singing what he calls "theologically lightweight" lyrics, neglecting "precious pearls of worship." Sarwar grew up singing seventy of Shahbaz's psalm portions at home and church, and when he discovered a complete 1905 Zaboor Psalter in Western notation, he determined to "preserve and transfer this great heritage and musical identity to coming generations," establishing the Tehillim School of Church Music and Worship.

But within a few months his work suddenly stopped, and Eric's friends received this email update:

> With regret we would like to inform you that Rev. Eric Sarwar (Minister of Presbyterian Church of Pakistan & Director of Tehillim School of Church Music and Worship) has been attacked in Karachi by unknown peoples. Attackers tried to kidnap him on gunpoint but due to his resistance, they failed

. . . he's been at the hospital since last night due to his injuries. Kindly pray for his safety and health as his family is still threatened and in danger.

How do you respond to such personal enemies, dragons who march from the margins of your life to threaten you at gunpoint? How do you pray when people beat up your pastor or kill your son, simply because he follows Jesus?

The psalms teach us that the best way to deal with enemies is not to fight them ourselves but to place them in God's hands by bringing them into our prayers. Over and over the psalmists pray about their enemies, asking God to "strike [their] enemies in the jaw" and "break the teeth of the wicked" (Psalm 3); to "banish them for their many sins" (Psalm 5). And in Psalm 7, the psalmist takes comfort that God is already armed for the conflict we face: "He will sharpen his sword; he will bend and string his bow. He has prepared his deadly weapons; he makes ready his flaming arrows." On and on the psalmists pray about their enemies, asking God to slay them, to call them to account for their wickedness.

Like Eric Sarwar, Dietrich Bonhoeffer seems a most unlikely person to collect powerful enemies. Born into a German family of high pedigree; both his parents counted highly distinguished and accomplished people among their ancestors. Bonhoeffer's father, Karl, was a highly regarded psychiatrist in Germany, his brother Klaus a top-ranking lawyer for the German airline Lufthansa, and his brother Karl-Friedrich an acclaimed scientist who worked with Albert Einstein on splitting the atom. When Dietrich announced his decision to study theology, his family was stunned. Why would he waste his life for something of so little consequence?

Undaunted, he earned his Ph.D. and seemed destined to become a captivating, thoughtful university professor. But his promising career was forever derailed when the Nazis came to power in Germany. From the start, Bonhoeffer became their determined opponent. In a radio address two days after Hitler was installed as chancellor, Bonhoeffer warned his fellow Germans against slipping into an idolatrous cult of any *Führer*. Such a leader, he said, could very well turn out to be the *Verführer* (seducer) instead. Bonhoeffer's radio speech, cut off the air mid-sentence, was never completed. A few months later, he raised a lonely plea for church-wide resistance to Hitler's persecution of the Jews, declaring that the church must not simply "bandage the victims under the wheel, but jam the spoke in the wheel itself."[15]

Outvoted and ignored in the state-run German Lutheran Church, Bonhoeffer helped form the "Confessing Church," a small collection of congregations that organized Christian opposition to Nazis. Not content to serve merely as an academic theologian, he pastored small congregations of German expatriates in Spain and London and helped teach Sunday school in Harlem as a visiting lecturer at a New York City seminary. Later he taught at Finkenwalde, an alternate seminary he helped establish while traveling from one eastern German town to another.

Centuries of culture and sturdy upbringing predisposed German Christians to honor their country and its leader as a sign of their faith. Even when confronted by warning signs that this new regime opposed basic Christian morality, many Christians sought to build goodwill with the

Nazis. The great majority of church leaders signed a loyalty oath to the Führer, many urged by their bishops and leaders. Some went further, reintroducing the ancient heretical practice of reducing the Old Testament to optional status for Christian teaching and practice. Everything Jewish was suspect, and eventually all but obliterated.

Even as German leaders were distancing themselves from the Jews, Bonhoeffer was accenting the Jewish roots of the Christian faith. In 1940 he published what would become his last book, *Das Gebetbook der Bibel* (*The Prayer Book of the Bible*). In it he affirmed the importance of the Old Testament for vital Christianity and church life, and he urged the church to use the Psalter as its prayer book. When we pray the psalms, he said, we "pray along with Christ's prayer and therefore may be certain and glad that God hears us."[16]

Under heavy scrutiny, *The Prayer Book* was considered politically subversive. Bonhoeffer knew that if he sent the manuscript to the Reich Board for the Regulation of Literature for approval, his book would never be published. Instead he claimed the book was "merely scholarly literary exegesis."[17] He believed that biblical truth would ultimately prevail over Nazi teaching in a way that bullets could not. The following spring he learned that his publishing career had ended. This small book caused the Nazis to forbid him from ever publishing again.

Bonhoeffer kept a keen eye on his enemies as Nazi power grew more sinister. In his role as a leader in the Confessing Church, many pastors watched his actions, using his example to shape their own actions. But Bonhoeffer was performing a sort of pastoral high-wire act, also assuming a double role as spy and counterspy. His sister-in-law Emmi prodded him toward serious involvement in plots against Hitler. "You Christians are glad when someone else does what you know must be done," she said, "but it seems that somehow you are unwilling to get your own hands dirty and do it."[18] Bonhoeffer carefully considered what she said, and eventually he crossed the line from "resisting by way of confession" to "confessing by way of resistance."

Bonhoeffer lived in a pivotal, tragic moment in history, a time when hell opened its doors and cheered as a thousand sinister demons spread their diabolical poison across the globe. Our time, by contrast, can seem dull and ordinary. But Bonhoeffer's courageous actions rose from his core belief that every Christian must be "fully human." Each must allow God into the center of his or her life, not just certain "spiritual" parts. Might the capacity to be fully human, to yield fully to God, be tied to the psalm-like practice of directly naming and facing our enemies?

––––––––––––

I once attended a pastors' retreat in a bucolic setting with fellow clergy, each wanting to deepen their ability to serve their church members. A veteran church leader and an astute psychiatrist led a session on "naming reality." In the church and in prayer, they said, Christians often deny reality. Afraid of anything the slightest bit negative, we angle toward the cult of "nice." We speak nice. We eat nice. We act nice. We live nice. Even when our "niceness" refutes reality.

Our retreat leaders urged us to think of members of our home congregations in animal terms. Every community, they suggested, includes peacocks and swans and bears and unicorns. Every community includes a snake or a donkey.

Church people who are afraid to name reality or to call a spade a spade may suggest that harmful people are not snakes but "lost souls" who are still "finding their way," not donkeys but beautiful stallions waiting to burst out of their disguise. Sometimes, said our leaders, this might be true. But many other times individuals who look like donkeys and smell like donkeys and bray like donkeys actually *are* donkeys—not "thoroughbreds" or "unicorns" in disguise. In the same way, if someone slithers like a snake, whispers slander like a snake, and regularly speaks malice from a forked tongue, it's time to name reality. Such a person is in fact a snake—often highly poisonous to the group. Failing to name insidious enemies within ultimately diminishes the community itself.

Might Bonhoeffer's high regard for the psalms and his practice of praying them—even those with dragons on the margins—be a key component of what enabled him to name the dark spiritual reality in the German church that duped so many well-intentioned saints?

Through his association with *Abwehr*, Bonhoeffer knew of various plots to assassinate Hitler, an involvement and knowledge that resulted in his arrest in April 1943. Writing his parents from his Nazi prison in May, he said, "I read the Psalms every day, as I have done for years; I know them and love them more than any other book. I cannot now read Psalms 3, 47, 70 and others without hearing them in the settings by Heinrich Schutz. . . . I count it one of the greatest enrichments of my life."[19] And in his *Prayer Book*, he wrote, "Wherever the Psalter is abandoned, an incomparable treasure vanishes from the Christian church. With its recovery will come unsuspected power."[20]

On April 9, 1945, just three weeks before the war's end, orders came from top-level German leaders to execute Bonhoeffer. Like other prisoners, Bonhoeffer was stripped naked and hung by wire. Ten years later, the camp doctor who witnessed his execution recalled, "I saw Pastor Bonhoeffer, before taking off his prison garb, kneeling on the floor praying fervently to God. I was most deeply moved by the way this unusually lovable man prayed, so devout and so certain that God heard his prayer. At the place of execution, he again said a short prayer and then climbed the few steps to the gallows, brave and composed. His death ensued after a few seconds. In the almost fifty years that I worked as a doctor, I have hardly ever seen a man die so entirely submissive to the will of God."[21]

Might Bonhoeffer have prayed Psalm 3 as he bowed naked, about to be hung? Or part of Psalm 119, his favorite psalm? He must have prayed the way he taught his students to pray, trusting that in praying God's own words we have full confidence that he listens.

Sarwar responded to his own attack by finding comfort in Psalm 18, "the most popular psalm in Pakistan. It represents God's providence, safety, power, deliverance, and kindness. In our context of living below the poverty line, fighting bigotry, and the agonizing challenges of everyday living, the psalm offers hope and encouragement. Its musical tune and rhythm is simple, catchy, and on high notes with shouts of joy."[22]

Psalms tell us the truth: enemies are everywhere. But they do not have the final word. The enemies who lurk like dragons on the margins of our lives and who let loose their toxic brew of hate and anger in the center of our lives are finally undone. Pray-ers brave enough to name their foes find new ways to hope. In the act of expressing disgust, fury, and spite to the Almighty, the psalmist moves toward trust, a trust that leads to obedience. Prayed fear and dread are re-wrapped in reliance.

PRONE TO WONDER

PSALM 8

"A Psalm is a tranquility of soul and the arbitration of peace; it settles one's tumultuous and seething thoughts. It mollifies the soul's wrath and chastens its recalcitrance. A psalm creates friendships, unites the separated, and reconciles those at enmity. Who can consider one to be a foe with whom one utters the same prayer to God!"[1]

—Basil

When I consider your heavens, the work of your fingers,
the moon and the stars, which you have set in place,
what is mankind that you are mindful of them,
human beings that you care for them?

—Psalm 8:3-4

The trajectory was all wrong. Four full seconds ahead of schedule, the current course was about to send the astronauts miles west of their meticulously planned target. Surface landmarks were passing too quickly. An alarm sounded, indicating that their navigation computer was no longer functioning. Or was it? Keenly aware of how a fraction of a second could critically affect their mission, they urgently radioed base: What should we do? Scrambling to examine the data as quickly and thoroughly as possible, support engineers determined that they could safely carry on. Their computer was fully functioning; its clanging alarms were only indicating a need to postpone certain tasks. But who really knew? No one had ever done this before.

Peering through thick triangular windows, the men spied their landing target, a boulder-strewn area just north and east of a giant crater. As their descent continued, Edwin Aldrin constantly relayed navigation data to the lunar module's pilot. Then a probe hanging from a footpad touched the surface. "Contact light!" he radioed. Three seconds later, the lunar module *Eagle* landed. Back in Houston NASA officials acknowledged the first humans on the moon: "We copy you down, *Eagle*." After completing his post-landing checklist, fellow astronaut Neal Armstrong spoke his famous words, "Houston, Tranquility Base here. The *Eagle* has landed."

Engineers and officials back at Houston's Mission Control shouted their relief and joy. A nation's dream was now an incredible reality: a human was on the moon. Elaborately rehearsed plans called for the astronauts to take a five-hour nap. But who could sleep after landing on the moon? Instead, the pair began preparing for what jargon-loving NASA officials labeled EVA (for extra-vehicular activity)—what most earthlings called the first moon walk.

A planet full of people wondered as black-and-white images relayed from the surface of the moon. Unseen by any of the 600 million viewers and unknown to NASA engineers, Aldrin withdrew the bag he had hidden in his stowage pouch. Setting a small flask of wine, a chalice, and some wafers on a fold-down table, he then celebrated the communion prepared by his pastor back home on planet Earth. He could imagine no better way to celebrate the sacrament.

Preparations for the moon walk took longer than scheduled. Engineers had redesigned *Eagle*'s module opening but not the space suit astronauts wore when stepping through that opening. Eventually Armstrong squeezed through, climbing down *Eagle*'s nine-rung ladder. Setting his left foot on the moon's surface, Armstrong uttered his now legendary words: "That's one small step for man, one giant leap for mankind." Aldrin soon joined him, describing the breathtaking view from the moon as "magnificent desolation."

After *Eagle* pushed off the moon's surface and rendez-voused with *Columbia*, the Apollo 11 astronauts each relayed carefully selected messages to the enraptured humans watching from their home planet. Michael Collins affirmed the "blood, sweat, and tears" of countless people who had worked to put the astronauts into orbit. Armstrong thanked those who "did the construction, design, and the tests and put their hearts and all their abilities into those craft." Aldrin added, "This has been far more than three men on a mission to the Moon; more, still, than the efforts of a government and industry team; more, even, than the efforts of one nation. We feel that this stands as a symbol of the insatiable curiosity of all mankind to explore the unknown. . . . Personally, in reflecting on the events of the past several days, a verse from Psalms comes to mind: 'When I consider the heavens, the work of Thy fingers, the Moon and the stars, which Thou hast ordained; What is man that Thou art mindful of him?'"[2]

Whether it's the solar system or an unknown continent, humans seem to have exploration in their DNA. Born in Berlin in 1769, Alexander Von Humboldt was his own phenomenon. His expertise knew no bounds: he was at once an astronomer, naturalist, botanist, geologist, and geographer. In the words of the poet Goethe, Humboldt was an "academy unto himself."[3] Admirers called him the "high priest of natural science." World-renowned scholars and scientists traveled thousands of miles to meet him. He so inspired Charles Darwin that on the voyage of the *Beagle*, Darwin brought three inspirational books: the Bible, the poetry of Milton, and Humboldt.

After decades of denying entry to all foreigners, Spain granted Humboldt and his companion Bonpland permission to explore the vast and uncharted territories of its colonial holdings in the Americas. So in 1799 he sailed for Cuba. When a typhoid outbreak shifted the ship's landing plans, Humboldt's party and his scientific instruments were set ashore on the coast of New Grenada (what we know now as Venezuela). Landing in this lush South American world, Humboldt's enthusiasm was boundless. Every plant, every creature was new. "We are here in a divine country," he wrote to his brother. "What trees! Coconut trees, fifty to sixty feet high, *Poinciana pulcherrima*, with a foot-high bouquet of magnificent bright-red flowers . . . and what colors in birds, fish, even crayfish (sky blue and yellow)! . . . Bonpland keeps telling me that he will go mad if wonders do not cease soon."[4]

The wonders did not cease. Overflowing with awe, Humboldt took notes as bountiful as his subjects: tides, soils, chocolate and rubber, turtle eggs, howling monkeys and alligators, vampire bats and electric eels. Humboldt became known as the second Columbus, mapping entire regions, collecting sixteen hundred plant specimens alone, and exploring river mouths. He and Bonpland witnessed a total eclipse of the sun, a spectacular meteor shower that went on for hours, and survived an earthquake.

As he traveled thousands of miles through one of the most difficult and little-known places on earth, nothing escaped his notice or his sense of wonder. Even when almost eaten alive by mosquitoes, he marveled at what he called the "harmony of nature." After becoming America's most renowned late nineteenth century naturalist, Humboldt's student Louis Agassiz would declare, "Humboldt is not only an observer, not only a physicist, a geographer, a geologist of matchless power and erudition; he knows that nature has its attraction for the soul of man."[5] Some scientists, then and now, believed that a "robust and thorough study of nature" would reduce its magic and mysteries. Humboldt called such a view narrow-minded and sentimental. Rather, he said, an exact study of the world only made its wonders more enthralling.[6]

In his exhaustive exploration of the psalms, Charles Haddon Spurgeon, a nineteenth century mega-church pastor in London, quotes Humboldt in his notes on Psalm 8:3:

When I consider . . . the moon and the stars . . . :
the mere thought they are so far beyond and
above everything terrestrial—the feeling, that
before them everything earthly so utterly vanishes
to nothing—that the single man is so infinitely
insignificant in the comparison with these worlds
strewn over all space—that his destinies, his enjoy-
ments, and sacrifices, to which he attaches such a
minute importance—how all these fade like nothing before such immense objects; then, that the
constellations bind together all the races of man,
and all the eras of earth, that they have beheld all
that has passed since the beginning of time, and
will see all that passes until its end; in thoughts like
these I can always lose myself with a silent delight
in the view of the starry firmament. It is, in very
truth, a spectacle of the highest solemnity. . . .[7]

A generation of North American explorers caught
Humboldt's zeal for exploring. When a young man named
Jedediah Smith saw an advertisement in the *Missouri
Gazette* calling for "young men of enterprise," he responded
immediately. Craving adventure, Smith leaped at the
chance to join the new fraternity of mountain men and
trappers venturing into the underexplored wilderness of
the American West. Having dreamt of such a life since
reading the *Journals of Lewis and Clark*, Smith led expedi-
tions in the Rockies, Oregon's Columbia River, Nevada's
Great Basin, and all through the Sierra Nevada mountain
range. Historian John Moring wrote that Smith covered
more territory on foot and on horseback and experienced

more adventure than anyone in his era,[8] all the while filling his journals with detailed descriptions of nature's marvels.

Beyond his incredible physical stamina, what made Smith stand out was his loyalty to his Methodist upbringing. "[H]e carried his Bible with him . . . and he was fond of singing gospel songs while riding. . . . He didn't smoke or curse, and he resisted the temptations of Indian women in the mountains. Smith's behavior was unheard of among the fraternity of mountain men. To confuse the other trappers even more, Smith was clean-shaven and he bathed regularly."[9]

The 2005 television miniseries *Into the West* captures Smith's regard for life. One scene has Smith's expedition party meeting a friendly village of Mohave people. After an afternoon of trading, most of the trappers settle in for a night of drinking and carousing. A novice mountain man is about to join in when he considers Smith. Searching the huts, the camp, and then the hillsides, he finds Smith alone on a ridge. "I want to be like you," he says, adding, after a moment's reflection, "Aren't you tempted like the other men?" Smith responds with words from Psalm 8, that God has "fashioned us a little lower than the angels," and then offers this commentary: "Humans are great, and weak. . . . Some men come west and lose their souls . . . but the west is a place on a map, not a way to live."[10]

Psalm 8 expresses a faith anchored in the wonders we see in the creation. Its opening and closing lines celebrate God and the splendor we see in the universe. The inner lines celebrate the wonder of human beings, the center and focus of God's creative work. "What is mankind that you are mindful of them?" asks the psalmist. The astounding answer is that humans, like God, are marked with glory and honor; they even play a key role in directing the universe. The psalmist praises God, who made humans "rulers over the works of your hands" and "put everything under their feet" (verse 6). Psalm 8 is a song to human dignity.

In the late 1700s and early 1800s, slavery was a long-standing historical institution. What's more, many British politicians were convinced that it was an institution on which the well-being of the empire depended. While regretting the unfortunate mistreatment of slaves, they believed that without slavery the empire would crumble. And who could bear the thought of British subjects speaking French, or Portuguese?

In his book *Bury the Chains,* Adam Hochschild points out that slavery's profits were a primary path to respectability. John Gladstone, father of a future prime minister, owned Caribbean estates with well over a thousand slaves. The cathedral-like library in Oxford's All Souls College was financed by the work of slaves in Barbados, as was the work of Edward Colston, a member of Parliament and the best-known philanthropist in Bristol. Colston lavished money on schools and poorhouses, hospitals, and lodging for retired seamen, proudly declaring that "every helpless widow is my wife and her distressed orphans my children." To this day a large bronze statue of Colston stands in downtown Bristol. In 1998 someone scrawled on its base the profession by which he made his fortune: Slave trader.[11]

Christians were not exempt from participating in slavery. We can revisit the horror and degradation of slavery during that time because one Barbados seaside plantation, Codrington, kept unusually thorough records of slave life. Its 710 acres of rich red soil and plentiful rainfall were perfect for a first-rate crop of sugar. In the great house lived a resident manager and his assistants, attended by nineteen slaves. Another 250 field slaves planted cane shoots in holes dug by hand. They chopped and carried bundles of cane to the mill, working in unbearable heat and afflicted by mosquitoes and disease. After their field work was done, slaves often worked an additional night shift in the "boiling house," where they were "very apt to get scalded" as profit-craving managers kept their mills going all year long. By all accounts work in the sugar fields was brutal, far more so than in the American South. The life of even the most obedient slave was very short. Careful clerks recorded the slaves' causes of death along with those of cattle, hogs, and horses. Causes included "a flux," "convulsed," and "shot by Accident." Because running away was a constant temptation, officials branded all slaves on their chests. The absentee owner of this plantation was the Church of England.[12]

It was not uncommon for sailors or captains to talk theology on the deck of a ship with hundreds of slaves chained and stacked like cordwood in the hold. When opposition to slavery surfaced, plantation owners tried to maintain some semblance of public respectability by inventing new titles for slaves, calling them "Assistant Planters," much like our own practice of calling store clerks "associates." In the United States many southern ministers owned slaves, including as many as 40 percent of Baptist ministers in South Carolina just before the Civil War.

The problem for abolitionists was that they couldn't find any biblical texts condemning slavery. In the American South, Christians often quoted passages from the Old and New Testaments that they believed condoned the institution, including Paul's admonition to slaves to "obey your earthly masters in everything" (Colossians 3:22) and to "consider [your] masters worthy of full respect" (1 Timothy 6:1). To southern slave owners, Paul never specifically rejected slavery but only "Christianized" it. It seemed perfectly clear to them that the institution of slavery would continue forever.

Thankfully abolitionist pastors and theologians found wisdom in the broad themes of the Bible. Slavery, they argued, violated Jesus' command to love our neighbors as ourselves. It worked against human dignity. In his groundbreaking book *The Bible Against Slavery,* published in 1837, Theodore Weld enumerates how Psalm 8, with its emphasis on the glory of humans, sharply contrasts with the way slavery destroys human dignity:

(1.) *"Thou hast made him a little lower than the angels."* Slavery drags him down among brutes. (2.) *"And hast crowned him with glory and honor."* Slavery tears off his crown, and puts on a yoke. (3.) *"Thou madest him to have dominion over the works of thy hands."* Slavery breaks his scepter, and casts him down among those works—yea, beneath them.[13]

Slaves didn't need Weld's book to come to the same conclusion. When churches sent missionaries to plantations—not to preach against slavery but to make nice Christians of them—slaves began learning to read and write. They could attain positions of respect, such as deacon or elder. They could be part of a multinational fellowship. And they couldn't help but notice how the vision of human dignity proclaimed in the Bible contrasted fundamentally with slavery. This biblical truth began to electrify slaves and missionaries alike: "It was easy most unintentionally to err," wrote Reverend Hope Waddell, a young Presbyterian who arrived in Jamaica in 1829, "and to say things in a slave congregation fit only for a free one." No wonder the presence of these Baptist, Presbyterian, Moravian, and Methodist missionaries eventually enraged the plantation owners. "Police had several times found excuses to briefly throw some of them in jail, and one missionary's house was shot at."[14]

The practice of psalm singing in particular stirred a new and deep sense of dignity for slaves by providing a way for them to voice their oppression and lament. But psalms also helped slaves to recognize their rightful place in the universe as human beings "a little lower than the angels." Like oil in a seized bolt, the gospel of the psalms worked its gracious message of human dignity into the hearts and minds of slaves, and even into some of their owners.

Psalms scholar James L. Mays says that Psalm 8 holds together the two dominant questions every generation asks: "Who is God?" and "Who are humans?" In answering the first question, the psalm offers its own unambiguous answer to the second.[15]

Who are we? What is our place in the universe? Slave traders saw humans as means of profit, as possessions to be bought and sold. Advertisers see humans as consumers always on the verge of making another purchase. Descartes famously described humans as rational beings: "I think, therefore I am." Some screenplays portray humans as predators with a natural instinct to kill. Sigmund Freud viewed people as sexual creatures, often acting out of repressed urges. But anyone who has visited Disneyland or watched a Disney movie with their kids, as I have, knows the truth: We are princes and princesses.

Enchanted is a movie conglomeration of classic Disney themes. Lost and removed from her home in Andalasia, the fairy-tale princess Giselle magically and mysteriously falls into the real life hustle of downtown Manhattan. Naïvely accepting people's words, she waltzes and sings her way through the city, taking every billboard message in Times Square at face value. When a bag lady in Central Park asks for a handout, Giselle gives her all her money. She treats stray animals with unfailing courtesy and decorum. Giselle believes in compassion, generosity, and kindness. But like every animated princess, Giselle believes above all in the power of love, symbolized in a true love's kiss. Her fundamental assumption—and every little girl's dream—is that she is a princess. In the land of fairy tales, we're all kings and queens just one true kiss away from being deeply loved. We're all a little lower than the angels.

Could it be that *Enchanted* actually resonates with a biblical understanding of personhood? Could it be that every human, even the most mistreated, carries within an ancient knowledge of our race that resonates with Psalm 8's vision: that we bear the image of God? That question is everywhere, just beneath the surface. And always, it seems, we are trying to answer it. In 1863 Oxford scientist T. H. Huxley wrote, "The question of all questions for humanity, the problem which lies beyond all others and is more interesting than any of them, is that of the determination of man's place in nature and his relation to the cosmos. Whence our race came, what sorts of limits are set to our power over nature and to nature's power over us, to what goal we are striving are the problems which present themselves afresh with undiminished interest to every human being on earth."[16] Those words ring with even more relevance as we stumble into the twenty-first century.

One year, during their spring concert, our local high school choir director and hard-working students took the audience on a wide-ranging musical expedition. It included the haunting "Zigeunerleben" by Schumann in German, the Irish classic "Danny Boy," the spiritual "Rockin' Jerusalem," the finale from the musical *Rent*, and "The Sound of Silence" by Simon and Garfunkel. A senior choir member introduced each song for the audience, giving us its historical context and musical setting. I winced when they explained "The Sound of Silence." Can so many years have gone by that we need historical context for Simon and Garfunkel?

A favorite feature of the concert is the moment when the seniors announce the song they've chosen as their "class song." This year it was "Go the Distance" from the Disney movie *Hercules*. Full of poise and brimming with self-confidence, a student explained, "We chose this song because we grew up with the musical and because there really is a god in each of us." I winced again. A god in each of us? In that public setting, this student professed her answer to the ancient questions "Who are we as humans?" and "What's our role in the universe?" Was her statement just the enthusiasm of an eighteen-year-old drinking that heady mix of nostalgia and keenly anticipated freedom that descends on pre-graduation high school seniors? Or was she giving voice to a misperception embedded in our entire culture? Might her phrase show that we've dropped one of the psalm's two questions? Do we think so highly of ourselves that we've lost our balance?

Ten days after the choir concert, the high school seniors reprised "Go the Distance" as part of their graduation ceremony. Earlier the valedictorian had cheered on his peers with his version of the classic "we can do anything" speech, after which the high school principal had enthused, "This is the greatest class in the history of this high school." To prove his point, the principal recited a litany of class successes, pointing to league championships in football, baseball, basketball, and women's volleyball. He recounted academic achievements, listing the feats of several valedictorians, and highlighted students with stellar SAT prowess, including my daughter's perfect SAT score in math. Then the choir sang the school song, which includes the line "we are among the nation's finest."

I couldn't help wondering if the message of this graduation ceremony might surpass even the heights of human glory affirmed by this psalm. It is a pastor's curse, I suppose, to be thinking theologically during a daughter's graduation ceremony. Couldn't I give it a rest for eighty minutes? Shouldn't a parent swell with pride—or at least breathe relief that a son or daughter has graduated? Isn't this the time for civic pleasure: "Look at all these wonderful young people, our country is in such good hands," or competitive pride: "My child is going to UC Berkeley; how about yours?"

My thoughts detoured back six years to my son's eighth grade "promotion" (the word "graduation" was deemed inappropriate). That too had been a long shower of unending self-congratulation. I'll grant you, any person who survives two years among six hundred seventh and eighth graders, navigating that hotbed of hormones and pecking orders while retaining a shred of normalcy, is well deserving of kudos. Bathed in the language of self-esteem, awards were given for the best math student, the best science student, the most athletic, the most popular. Students paraded to the stage in groups, in trios, in pairs, and solo. Each presentation was followed by a fresh soaking of impromptu esteem-building phrases like "You are wonderful," "You are talented," "You are gifted," and "We like you."

As I eyed the crowd of self-absorbed suburban adolescents, I doubted that any of them lacked a well-developed sense of self. I had witnessed many of these kids on the soccer field, on the basketball court, and walking to school. Did these kids have any sense of "Other"? Sure, I remember firsthand how masterfully junior high students mask their insecurity with bravado. But that day I found myself thinking, "Really? Is this is the best we have to offer these kids? Is this dunking exercise in self-esteem the best way to ready a person for high school? Isn't it enough to be "a little lower than the angels"? Do we need to be above them?

In time my wandering thoughts looped back to the white plastic seat where I sat on the high school's football field. Four hundred students were graduating. Listening to each name called left plenty of time for side trips down theological alleyways. I had so much to be thankful for: the event had started on time, the temperature was less than 90 degrees, the band played a John Philip Sousa march with style, and the oratory of the eighteen-year-old speakers was impressive. Most of all, my daughter was graduating. Many of these students deserved their accolades. But what about the disabled seniors who had bumped along the football field in their wheelchairs and then down an aisle too narrow for them to go side by side like their walking peers? And what about their parents?

I was sitting in the reserved section; each graduate in the greatest class in school history was given two seats in this closer-to-the-action section. Three rows in front of me a couple of grandparents stood up to search for their granddaughter among the graduates. They wanted to catch a good photo of her as she walked across the stage 50 yards away. So they stood. And they kept standing, holding their cameras and pointing. After fifteen seconds other parents hissed, "Sit down. We want to see too!" Undeterred or unhearing, the grandparents stood their ground. Life isn't always easy among the nation's finest.

I wondered again about Buzz Aldrin's words from the space ship *Columbia* as he circled the moon. What if, following his lead, we gave graduates, astronauts, Oscar winners, World Series champions, and new parents hand-written notes of congratulations and best wishes, along with the text of Psalm 8?

QUESTION MARKS

PSALM 13

"Words and music did for me what solid, even rigorous, religious argument could never do—they introduced me to God, not belief in God, more an experiential sense of GOD. . . . As a result, the Book of Psalms always felt open to me."[1]

—Bono

How long, LORD? Will you forget me forever?
How long will you hide your face from me?
How long must I wrestle with my thoughts
and day after day have sorrow in my heart?
How long will my enemy triumph over me?
Look on me and answer, LORD my God.
Give light to my eyes, or I will sleep in death,
and my enemy will say, "I have overcome him,"
and my foes will rejoice when I fall.

But I trust in your unfailing love;
my heart rejoices in your salvation.
I will sing the LORD's praise,
for he has been good to me.

—Psalm 13

My neighbor and I are longtime friends. Sometimes he begins our conversations. Sometimes I do. We talk about bikes and sports and weather. In California weather can be a short conversation—sunny *again*. Sometimes we don't feel like talking, so we just wave. A while back he and his mom knocked on our front door. They were holding hands. This isn't so unusual, since my neighbor is in kindergarten. When my wife greeted them, they asked for me. Caleb's mother began, "Caleb has a question for you." Then Caleb dropped his bombshell: "Where do people come from?"

My kindergarten friend knocked me off balance. We ask each other questions all the time: How's it going? What are you doing for Halloween? How was school today? But this was different. My first reaction was to pull his mom aside and say, "You can't get off this easy. Parents are supposed to teach their children about reproduction." But when I replayed his question in my mind, I realized that my young friend wasn't asking where babies come from but where *people* come from. Caleb wanted to talk theology.

A few years earlier his mom had knocked on our door with a different question. "Would you officiate at my dad's funeral?" I'd known her dad for years. He and his wife babysat their grandkids regularly, and he was a neighborhood favorite. A sucker for every child-sponsored fund raiser, he'd buy candy, raffle tickets, books with discount coupons—any of the overpriced stuff schools coax their students to sell. The bar had been open for some time when I arrived at his backyard memorial service. Mountain folk raised in the California foothills filled the yard. I was smitten with their lack of pretense and their deep loyalty to their friend and his family. They swapped stories with each other and the family; a few stood to publicly share their favorite tales of Tom. Pointing to me at the end of his memorial speech, one man asked, "How did you find a man of the cloth who knew Tom? I had no idea he knew a pastor."

Six months after her dad's funeral Caleb's mom knocked on my door again. Would I preside at her grandpa's funeral? Now Caleb's family knocks on my door with all their God questions. So there Caleb stood, wide-eyed and earnest, searching for answers.

Some questions are easier to answer than others. The book *Amazing Questions Kids Ask about God* is pitched as a "must-have reference tool for every parent and Sunday school." The book promises to arm parents with "thoughtful answers" to questions kids ask about God, heaven, and the Bible—questions like "Is there a McDonald's in heaven?" "What do angels really look like?" As a bonus, publishers say, the book is written in kid friendly language and supplemented with pictures. Pictures of a McDonald-less heaven or a reliable portrait of angels?

The questions tossed my way usually seem way too dicey for encyclopedic treatment with child-appropriate photos. Each is an original. It is as if the toddler's matchless questions never go away but only become increasingly complicated. Maybe we humans are destined to spend our whole life seeking answers to the first question we ask: Why?

When elementary-age children help to lead worship at my church, they often sit next to me before they go "on stage." Almost always they have questions: What comes next? When will the singing end? Is it my turn now? One extra-precocious kid set a record number for questions:

Why does everyone come late to church? What language does God use to talk? Why don't *you* lead the singing? After walking to the front of the sanctuary he whispered, "Can I greet the people?" Then, in the bantering folksy style of a veteran talk show host, he asked the congregation, "How's it going out there?"

Where *do* people come from?

Sometimes our children force us to ask desperate questions of ourselves. By North American standards John Van Sloten was living the good life. Funny, urbane, hip, he was a deal-making developer riding Toronto's real-estate boom, enjoying the status symbols that went with success. At work, he says, he was a bully, bulldozing architects and consultants. When thick-skinned contractors wrote to his boss to complain, the boss responded by giving John a bonus. He was so hard on one electrical engineer that the man ended up having a mental breakdown. At home John was equally caustic and vain. He was "constantly engrossed" with his net worth. "All I ever thought about was the next deal, the next car, the next house, and, sadly, even the next wife."[2] Then his wife gave birth to a son with Down syndrome.

John writes, "I started to run scenarios of how rotten being the father of a retarded child was going to be (sorry, no political correctness yet). I imagined going to church that Sunday and having to tell the entire community about my disabled boy. How would I be able to talk about him when I wasn't even sure that I could love him?" Other scenarios, each with their own questions, followed. When I take him bowling, will it have to be with other disabled kids in a place where they'll put bumpers in the gutters because no one can throw a ball straight? Will he have any friends when he's eighteen, or will he sit all alone in the corner of the high school cafeteria? When I'm dead, will he rot unloved and uncared for in some horrible institution?[3] After a lifetime of attending church, hearing hundreds of sermons, and singing thousands of hymns, in his moment of crisis all John had were questions.

I ordered my mother-in-law out of a catalogue. Who could find a prize like her? She drove a pick-up at the ranch, enjoyed watching ESPN, and grilled us steaks for dinner. She even laughed at my jokes. Decades before our marriage, when my wife was a four-year-old girl, Mom was diagnosed with breast cancer. My wife remembers her dad's brave attempt to dress his only daughter for church— on one occasion he managed to get her clothed, but she arrived with her Sunday dress on backward. When Mom won the first round of her fight with cancer her family breathed relief. But they always wondered when it would return. Thoughts about her cancer lingered for a long time, and then slowly faded. Twenty years later, when her first episode was all but forgotten, the cancer reappeared. This time it attacked her bones, breaking them from the inside. The afternoon we told her we were pregnant with our first child, she burst into tears. She was painfully aware that she would not live to see our first baby (later it turned out that none of us would, our first three pregnancies ended in miscarriage).

Mom battled her persistent enemy bravely, suffering chemo with charm and traveling as much as the pain would allow. There were good days—days she worked at the chicken ranch, days she walked along a Hawaiian beach, days she played with her granddaughter at a local pool. But the cancer was winning. Her body grew thin and weak.

Increasingly frail, she stayed in the hospital bed we placed in the family room. Her breathing became increasingly labored and shallow. Drifting in and out of consciousness during her final hours, she grabbed at her wedding ring, desperate to remove it. Ever practical, she didn't want to be buried with gold on her finger. One morning she raised her head, looked around with renewed alertness and asked, "Am I *still* here?" Her question reignited the intensity of ours. Why?

Like my mother-in-law, like John Van Sloten, like each of our suffering friends, we come to God with questions. We always have. Each heartfelt inquiry is our own. But each finds a soul mate in the psalms. Questions pour from the psalms like oil from an untamed deep-water well: Who praises you from the grave? (Psalm 6). Why, Lord, do you stand far off? (Psalm 10). Why do you hide yourself in times of trouble? (10). Lord, who may dwell in your sanctuary? (Psalm 15). How long, Lord, will you look on? (Psalm 35). Why, my soul, are you downcast? Why so disturbed within me? (Psalm 42).

Psalm 13 begins with five: How long, Lord? Will you forget me forever? How long will you hide your face from me? How long must I wrestle with my thoughts and day after day have sorrow in my heart? How long will my enemy triumph over me?

Our questions are as original as our fingerprints. But sometimes entire groups or generations share the same questions. During the Great Depression children and their parents wondered, "Will there be food on the table?" During the frightening early days of WWII people asked, "Will our world be ruled by villains? During the Cold War in the 1950s, American and Russian school children practiced hiding under their desks, wondering, "Will our world end with a mushroom cloud?" In the 1960s flower children asked, "Will they give peace a chance?"

Depleted of creative energy, with forty minutes of studio time remaining, the band U2 felt stuck. Bassist Adam Clayton had already left, and those who remained were searching for a song to close their album *War*. Lead singer Bono remembers, "We wanted to put something explicitly spiritual on the record." The band found their thoughts turning to the psalms, particularly Psalm 40. But they felt squeamish—unspoken rules prohibited rock groups from raiding Bible texts for lyrics. They did it anyway. The result was "40," a song full of questions.

Years after their impromptu psalm singing session, Bono expressed his affection for the psalms: "How do you explain a love and logic at the heart of the universe when the world is so out of kilter?" The psalms offered words from kindred spirits. How could he resist the work of the psalmist whose music was medicine to still the moody demons of King Saul? Bono remembers becoming a fan of David and his psalms at the age of twelve. They felt like the blues, he said. People shouted at God. They spoke their questions: "My God, my God, why hast thou forsaken me? Why art thou so far from helping me?" (Psalm 22). Bono prized the psalms' honesty, the way their questions roar with anger. "How long, Lord? Wilt thou hide thyself forever?" Psalms, he said, primed him for the "honesty of John Lennon, the baroque language of Bob Dylan and Leonard Cohen, the open throat of Al Green and Stevie Wonder"— singers who echo the psalms. In the words of "un-holy bluesman" Robert Johnson, "There's a hellhound on my trail," or Van Morrison, "Sometimes, I feel like a motherless child," Bono hears the psalms. "Words and music did for me what solid, even rigorous, religious argument could never do—they introduced me to God, not belief in God, more an experiential sense of GOD. . . . As a result, the Book of Psalms always felt open to me."[4]

The song "40" debuted live on February 26, 1983. For the next several years it became the way U2 closed their concerts. During performances band members left the stage one at a time while enthusiastic crowds continued to chant the refrain at full volume: How long to sing this song?

Jesus' first band of twelve disciples followed him, expecting answers to their questions. Who sinned, this man or his parents? Who is greatest in the kingdom of heaven? Is this the time you will restore the kingdom? We go to church or open a Bible for similar reasons, expecting professional clergy or church veterans to untangle our spiritual confusion. Religious experts who can't provide answers are considered ill-equipped or unfit for ministry. My kindergarten neighbor already has his favorite spiritual answer man. But maybe U2 concert-goers are on to something. Are questions themselves essential ingredients of faith?

At the ripe old age of eight I began weekly catechism instruction. In the church where I grew up, attending weekly Sunday school, two Sunday worship services, youth choir practice, and Christian day school was deemed insufficient religious training for school-age children. So one afternoon each week my fellow third-graders and I hustled the four blocks from school to church to learn the catechism. There we memorized questions and their four-hundred-year-old answers from the Heidelberg Catechism.

No third grader I knew was ready for either. Some of those question and answer combinations are extraordinarily beautiful: "What is your only comfort in life and in death? I am not my own but belong—body and soul, in life and in death—to my faithful Savior Jesus Christ. . . ." (Q&A 1). But I confess that when parroting it as a child its beauty escaped me.

Catechism instruction never did top the list of desirable activities for me or my third-grade friends. It was just something you did, not something you questioned. Our parents had participated in the same ritual. It was a rite of growing up, like bad haircuts and acne. Teachers and students alike assumed it would take years for each fresh crop of young disciples to see the wisdom of the catechism's theologically precise questions and answers. But most of the questions were miles beyond my mental capacity at eight years old and generated little of my interest: How does the holy conception and birth of Christ benefit you? (Q&A 36). Are we so corrupt that we are totally unable to do any good and inclined toward all evil? (Q&A 8). If [Christ's] humanity is not present wherever his divinity is, then aren't the two natures of Christ separated from each other? (Q&A 48). Do those who look for their salvation and security in saints, in themselves, or elsewhere really believe in the only savior Jesus? (Q&A 30).

My friends and I felt no pull to learn the wide-sweeping implications of the virgin birth or the precise applications of all the Ten Commandments, let alone join intramural sixteenth-century debates on Jesus' bodily presence in communion or the role of saints in prayer. We didn't suspect we would be attending Catholic services soon, and on the off chance we did, had little desire to know the difference between their mass and our Lord's Supper. Our eight-year-old theological questions were closer to my neighbor Caleb's. Why are the sermons so long? Why does the preacher use so many big words? Why can't we play baseball on Sundays? Will I ever play right field for the Detroit Tigers?

Still, each Wednesday afternoon after school, following in the footsteps of our fathers and mothers of faith, we hurried to church to learn the catechism's carefully scripted questions and answers. And our teachers and pastors bet that our youthful, if undesired, memorization would shape us for a lifetime of faith. Often they were right.

Only years later did I realize that while I was studying catechism, thousands of college students were ditching class to ask their own unscripted questions. University campuses and city streets thronged with people shouting and chanting questions that were unrehearsed and original with an agonizing overflow of zeal and passion.

Why this war? Why now? Why would a National Guardsman shoot into a throng of college protestors? Where have all the young men gone? When will they ever learn?

Churchgoers tend to be polite and staid. We like our religion organized. When we bring questions into the halls of faith we prefer to have them scripted, often with hundreds of years' advance notice. But like untamed college students of the 1960s, the psalms roar their questions. The psalms bootleg their untidy emotions inside the establishment. They suggest that worship, front and center, is the place for questions. But few churches or pastors train for this.

Pastors go to seminary to prepare for answering a lifetime of questions. Veteran believers order study Bibles and take online courses, hoping to gain theological competence and understanding of the answers collected by generations of Bible students. People treat the Bible like a medicine chest for everything that ails us or like an encyclopedia packed with God-facts. On television, online, in the streets, in the church, people spout answers to our questions: "God helps those who help themselves." "Five foolproof ways to affair-proof your marriage." "Three principles for raising 'G'-rated kids in an 'X'-rated world."

But real life is more complicated and confusing than our practiced answers presume.

At some level in our souls we are both believers and unbelievers. We believe. Sure we do. But sometimes, in a crunch, our belief morphs into questions—heated, heartfelt, heavy-hearted questions. We feel like Mary did when Jesus came to her brother Lazarus's tomb: "If you had been here, my brother would not have died" (John 11:21). Every person who has ever grieved knows Mary was really asking, "Why didn't you get here sooner?"

Could it be that our faith deepens when we ask questions? If we want our faith to increase, wouldn't it be wise to follow in the way of Jesus, who was taught the psalms from an early age? Saturated in their poetry, majesty, and theology, Jesus used the psalmists' words to pray for daily bread, to remember God's saving work, and to ask questions. In the darkest moment of his life, as he hung tormented on the cross, his voice strained to utter the haunting question from Psalm 22: "My God, my God, why have you forsaken me?

In wisdom stretching back hundreds of years, Eastern Orthodox believers pray Psalm 13 as a regular part of their Lenten litany. Often they pray it during Compline, the final service of the day. Before retiring for the night, they ask God their questions. The growing darkness outside symbolizes the enemy's power lurking. In that service, just before they go to bed, the monks ask God that their sleep will not be the sleep of death. Reflecting on this long-standing practice, Orthodox priest Patrick Reardon wonders if this psalm was in Jesus' mind that night in Gethsemane. The gospel of Luke records Jesus' words to his betrayer: "But this is your hour—when darkness reigns" (Luke 22:53). As Jesus battled that night, might he have prayed, "How long, O LORD? Will You abandon me forever? How long will You turn Your face away from me?"[5]

When life gets especially tenuous, even atheists speak a gut-wrenching "Why?" to a god they do not believe in. But believers ask questions *because* we trust that God is the one who answers. Psalms show us that we don't have to ask our questions from outside the faith or sequester them in a basement corner. Psalmists don't treat questions like expensive china to be used only on rare occasions. They pray their questions at every turn. Our anguished questions show us to be people of faith, people who still trust God in the chaos of life. We have no proof. We lack empirical data that anyone or anything in the universe will answer the question that rises from our misery. But still we pray our questions—Why? How long? When?

Questions may make us sound like skeptics, but in fact they show the depth of our trust. We question God without shyness. We accost God when his attention seems to be lacking. We complain about God to God. Psalms scholar James

Mays notes that some of our questions border on arrogance, even self-centeredness. But he encourages us to keep asking them. "It is more dangerous for faith to yield to isolation, to imagine that the experience of loneliness cannot be phrased in the language of devotion."[6]

Diet was a tomboy of seventeen when she met Hein. Uninterested in boys, she found the young man's conversation boring. It didn't compare to jovial weekends with her friends. But when Hein was drafted into the army and went away, she found herself missing him. Deeply. All of the Netherlands was afraid in 1938. Hitler had already taken control of Austria. When the Führer invaded Poland, Netherlanders knew things would get worse, and they did. In May 1940 Hitler's troops overwhelmed the Netherlands in five days.

So much of the military seemed a waste to Hein, yet his resistance was steady and brave. During the Nazi occupation, Diet and Hein became engaged. For the next six years they worked together in the underground. Thwarting the occupiers, risking their own safety and that of their friends, they hid Jewish people they had never met, saving hundreds of lives. Both Diet and Hein were eventually caught and imprisoned. From prison, they wrote letters to each other, using the smallest scraps of paper, even toilet paper when no other kind was available.

After the liberation, the Dutch came out of their hiding places. Bicycles and cars came back to life. Slowly freedom became their new reality. But there was still confusion—spouses and fiancés and siblings had been carried off by the occupiers. Where were they now? Feeling paralyzed, Diet and a friend whose husband was also missing tried to comfort each other with the psalms. They read to each other passages like Psalm 37: "The LORD makes firm the steps of the one who delights in him." One day a neighbor came to the front door of Diet's parents' home. In his hand he held a letter. Her fiancé had died four months earlier in Dachau. Writing in her diary after his death, she asked, "Why? Why did I have to come through it all? Why couldn't I also have died? Hein, why did you leave me alone? What am I going to do without you?"[7]

Trained by a church that prized the psalms, Diet knew that God wanted to hear her questions. Her painful questions echo those of her ancient teachers: Why did you forsake me? How long will you forget me? Sometimes all we have is questions. And sometimes questions lead us to the beginning of a divine reply.

Three months after the birth of Edward, his Down syndrome boy, John Van Sloten went on a weeklong trip to Rochester, New York. A year earlier he had promised to chaperone some teens from church. Now he wasn't in the mood. He didn't want to go. His wife was convinced it would be good for him, and finally he succumbed to her wisdom.

Their first night in town John's group attended a special event to welcome their team. Three rows back, John spotted what he took to be a forty-year-old man with Down syndrome and his frail-looking, gray-haired parents. He ran to his car and called his wife. "Obviously I'm not ready for this. . . . I think I should go home." His wife, a person of consistent kindness and compassion, told him to suck it up and get to work helping the group of teens that was counting on him.

When he reentered the building, the man with Down syndrome came right toward him. John remembers, "He introduced himself as Mark. Then he wrapped his arms around my waist, hugged me, and lifted me off the ground." When Mark's parents saw what their son was doing they rushed to John, now in tears, to apologize. When John recovered enough to explain the real reason for his tears, they sat down to talk. Mark's parents gave John "a different vision of what parenting a boy with disabilities could look like." Two days later, John met an eight-year-old Down syndrome boy whose mother could not stop talking about what a good boy he was. As she spoke, her son, also named Mark, kept showing John his muscles! Still later, he was introduced to Joe, an eighteen-year-old with Down syndrome. John's group was taking teens from Joe's home on a special trip to a local aquarium. John sat beside Joe, hoping to initiate a conversation. But Joe was far from interested. Why should he spend a day with strangers when he had plans to join a bunch of friends for a weekend getaway?

Driving home to Toronto the next day, John realized he missed his family, especially Edward. "If I'm missing Edward," he thought, "that must mean I love him." Tears came again at this unexpected answer to his anxious and earnest question. God knew. Fifteen years later John found himself praying a prayer he could not have imagined. He thanked God for the day of Edward's birth, for the way he had entered their lives. And suddenly he was overwhelmed with a new question, "How does it happen? How does what was once the worst day of your life become the best day of your life?"[8]

Eventually, in another surprise, astonishing his friends and family, John was called to be a preacher. He became the sort of preacher who encourages and listens to questions. Over the years he's found and preached God's presence in all kinds of unorthodox places: quantum physics, *The Lord of the Rings,* the movie *Crash,* a Stanley Cup playoff run, a World Cup soccer game, and *The Simpsons.* He's pointed to God's presence in disabilities, tattoos, Amy Winehouse, J. S. Bach, even Seven Card Texas Hold 'em. In each he sees God's mysterious ways in a specific part of the universe.

One Sunday morning, after John had preached a sermon on the band U2, a teen in his church asked, "Would you ever preach on a heavy metal band?" John's first response was "Never in a thousand years." But later that week a church-going novice called him at home. "Hey John. How are you doing? Listen, I've got two tickets for the Metallica concert this Thursday night and I was wondering if you and Fran would like to go?" John laughed out loud. Was this a divine conspiracy?

John did preach a sermon on Metallica, focusing especially on their questions. Were they actually questions of faith? "Who are you? Where ya been? Where ya from?/ Gossip burning on the tip of your tongue/You lie so much you believe yourself."[9] Could it be, John wondered with his congregation, that when Metallica denounces injustice and hypocrisy they're acting like Jesus clearing the money-changers out of the temple?

My friend Caleb still comes to my house with his questions. "Can I borrow a stapler?" "Would you like to buy raffle tickets from my Boy Scout troop?" "Want a piece of my birthday cake?" Occasionally he still asks the big ones. A few weeks ago he had a question his mom couldn't answer. "Let's go ask Kevin," he said. So there he was again, standing hand in hand with his mom beside my front door, his face full of innocence and wonder. "Why did God make the devil?" And before I could dare to answer, he asked, "Are people really going to go down there?"

TRANSFORMING BEAUTY

PSALM 27

*"There are only two things that can pierce the human heart: beauty
and affliction."*

—Simone Weil

*One thing I ask from the LORD, this only do I seek:
that I may dwell in the house of the LORD
all the days of my life,
to gaze on the beauty of the LORD
and to seek him in his temple.
For in the day of trouble
he will keep me safe in his dwelling;
he will hide me in the shelter of his sacred tent
and set me high upon a rock.
Then my head will be exalted
above the enemies who surround me;*

at his sacred tent I will sacrifice with shouts of joy;
I will sing and make music to the LORD.

—Psalm 27:4-6

They are a most unlikely pair. One has been well described as an "outsider's saint." The other is the ultimate insider. The first was raised by agnostic Jewish parents with no attention to spiritual formation. The second, the son and grandson of preachers, preached more than six hundred sermons before he became pastor of a famous London congregation at age twenty. Yet in distinct and overlapping ways, both were powerfully drawn to "the beauty of the Lord."

The "outsider's saint" was Simone Weil. Declining to be baptized, she wrote, "God does not want me in the church." At six years old she refused sugar to show her solidarity with the French troops entrenched along the Great War's Western Front. At ten she declared herself a Bolshevik. In her teens she joined a workers' movement and began writing political tracts and marching in demonstrations on behalf of workers' rights. As a young adult she left her teaching position to work incognito as a factory laborer to better understand working class people. Identifying herself as an anarchist, she fought in the Spanish Civil War despite her pacifism. After burning herself over a cooking fire, Weil was forced to leave Spain for Italy to recuperate. There she walked into the twelfth-century chapel of Santa Maria degli Angeli, where St. Francis often prayed. And was spiritually hijacked. For the first time in her life, she said later, she felt compelled to drop down on her knees.

The following April, suffering from constant migraine headaches, Weil visited the Benedictine monastery in Solesmes. For ten consecutive days she attended services, drinking in Gregorian chants, psalm after psalm. During those services, Weil said, "the thought of the Passion of

Christ entered into my being once and for all." Around that same time, a friend introduced Weil to the intoxicating beauty of seventeenth-century poetry. Weil would memorize and repeat lines of poetry as a kind of anesthesia to battle the pain of her migraines.

One of those poems was George Herbert's "Love." Lost in its verse—"'You must sit down,' says Love, 'and taste my meat.' So I did sit and eat"—Weil experienced a stunning, mystical encounter with Jesus. "Christ himself came down and took possession of me," she wrote. She felt "a presence more personal, more certain, and more real than that of any human being."[1] To her surprise, Herbert's poem had become in her a prayer. Through this mysterious spiritual awakening she recognized the "possibility of loving divine love in the midst of affliction."

Charles Spurgeon, the "insider," was a well-known preacher. Like Weil, he prized working class people. Addressing the church's tendency to discuss people's needs in committees rather than providing actual help, Spurgeon urged his students toward a radically different method of ministry, telling them to "do something, *do something*." Weil showed her solidarity with the working class by joining boycotts and fighting at their side; Spurgeon demonstrated his by preaching in a style that was accessible to them and spending himself on their behalf. As a preacher, he rejected clerical attire and ecclesiastical titles, focusing his energy instead on charitable causes. One such cause was the Stockwell Orphanage, which provided for 500 children. On his fiftieth birthday a friend read a list of sixty-six organizations that Spurgeon had founded and administered.[2]

These vast responsibilities were a calling he felt the gospel compelled him to do, but he also experienced them as a burden: "No one living knows the toil and care I have to bear. . . ." Like Weil, Spurgeon suffered intense physical pain throughout his adult life; in his case from rheumatism, Bright's disease, and gout. His first attack of gout came at the age of thirty-five, and each that followed caused increasing pain.

Weil distanced herself from the church because of what she saw as its disregard for the masses; Spurgeon's fellow clergymen distanced themselves from him by public slander. In April 1855, an article in the *Essex Standard* labeled Spurgeon's style "as that of the vulgar colloquial, varied by rant. . . . All the most solemn mysteries of our holy religion are by him rudely, roughly and impiously handled. Common sense is outraged and decency disgusted." A fellow London minister wrote, "Mr. Spurgeon's was a superlative egotism; not the shilly-shallying, timid, half-disguised egotism that cuts off its own head, but the full-grown, over-powering, sublime egotism that takes the chief seat as if by right. The only colors which Mr. Spurgeon recognized were black and white." Another added, "I have—most solemnly have—my doubts as to the Divine reality of his conversion."[3]

Besides battling physical ailments and attacks from fellow clergy, Spurgeon fought severe depression, which first struck him at the age of twenty-four—without warning, and seemingly without cause. It entered like a mist, he said, this "shapeless, indefinable, yet all-beclouding hopelessness" as a sort of "gloomy prison."[4]

In the psalms, both Spurgeon and Weil found words to both describe and comfort their suffering, strength to keep going, and beauty with power to give their lives meaning.

Both drew strongly on psalms in their prayer and in their writings.

For Weil, the psalms were a point of entry, a way to begin her journey to faith. At the beginning, navigating the Bible felt like a maze. Certain Old Testament passages— such as the divine instructions to kill every living being in the city of Amalek (1 Samuel 15) and the terrible miracle of Elisha's prophetic curse on the mischievous boys who jeered at his baldness (2 Kings 2:23-24)—shocked her almost beyond recovery. People who begin reading the Bible as children intuitively process such stories within the framework of their budding faith. But for those like Weil, who was reading the Bible for the first time in her late twenties, such passages cause profound alarm. In much of the Old Testament she saw the same blatant disregard for human life she found in the despicable regimes and "inhuman phenomena" of the twentieth century.[5] But the psalms were different. They displayed an honesty Weil found compelling and offered a beauty that could bring about renewal and transformation.

Lacking any conventionally structured spiritual practice, Weil sought reprieve for her misery in physical labor, in writing, and in focusing on the splendor she found in nature, in poetry, and in God himself. Beauty, she believed, was imbedded in creation—as evident in a solid mathematical equation as in "art of the very first order." Beauty is proof that the world points to something beyond itself; it is evidence that Jesus' incarnation was possible. Beauty experienced in nature and art, said Weil, is "a sensible reflection of the mystery of faith."

True beauty offers the possibility of true change, a sort of spiritual makeover. It offers a glimpse of true love. Weil glories, "I only felt in the midst of my suffering the presence of a love, like that which one can read in the smile on a beloved face."[6] In what could be a meditation on Psalm 27's longing "to gaze upon the beauty of the LORD," Weil wrote that beauty "captivates the flesh in order to obtain permission to pass right to the soul." She believed that divine reality invades our life through beauty. Meditating on Herbert's poem "Love" was a form of prayer that allowed her to meet God in a profound and tangible way. From personal experience, Weil understood that "the poet produces beauty by fixing his attention on something real."[7]

Was Weil's experience, shaped by her migraine headaches and a philosophical bent, unique? Or might any genuine encounter with beauty be a form of prayer, or, at least, the beginning of a prayer? Might all appreciation of and longing for beauty inch us heavenward, even if we don't believe in heaven? And could it work in either direction? In prayer, might you find yourself gazing on God's beauty? In gazing on beauty, might you find yourself praying?

Leonard Bernstein, composer of *West Side Story*, was a nihilist. He believed that ultimately all human life is empty and meaningless. A thoughtful biographer might suggest that this view was a result of living with his father, Sam, a Russian talmudic scholar who was destined to become a rabbi like his father—until he arrived in New York at age sixteen and began working twelve-hour days, six days a week, cleaning fish in the Lower East Side. Sam provided endless discouragement to Leonard's love for music. In 1958 Bernstein told the *New Yorker*: "Every genius had a handicap. Beethoven was deaf. Chopin had tuberculosis.

. . . someday the books will say, 'Leonard Bernstein had a father.'"[8]

But despite his nihilistic outlook, Leonard Bernstein's attitude toward music was one of unfettered and consummate love: "Life without music is unthinkable. Music without life is academic. That is why my contact with music is a total embrace." In music he experienced a boundless, joyful energy: "I can do things in the performance of music that if I did on an ordinary street would land me in jail. I can get rid of all kinds of tensions and hostilities. By the time I come to the end of Beethoven's Fifth, I'm a new man." His attitude was contagious: watching Bernstein, a cynical music veteran remarked, "When he gets up on the podium, he makes me remember why I wanted to become a musician." Is it possible that Bernstein's love of music was the beginning of a prayer, a prayer that finds voice in the psalmist's call to gaze on the "beauty of the Lord"? In music Bernstein had an encounter with beauty, a beauty beyond himself, a beauty that recreates and reorients us, giving us strength beyond our own.

Like Bernstein and Weil, another suffering "outsider" to organized religion found comfort in gazing on the beauty of the Lord. In April 1992, our fledgling congregation mailed out thousands of flyers inviting people to join us for our first worship service. We invited folks to take a risk on a new church meeting in a dilapidated warehouse in an abandoned section of town. We hoped a bit of fresh paint on the building might help potential attendees overcome the forbidding "No Outlet" sign posted just before our driveway. To our surprise, a couple of hundred people came. Gloria was one of them.

We invited folks to join one of four small groups in our new church. Each would be a place to form friendships, study the Bible, and ask questions about God. Gloria attended one of those groups, led by my wife and me. She came to a church she didn't know and visited a home she had never visited to study a Bible she barely knew. I had led many small groups before: college groups in Michigan and church groups in small-town Minnesota and in a burgeoning California city. I had been in groups with Mormons, plumbers, and bank presidents. I'd been in groups with Rush Limbaugh followers and liberal Democrats, construction supervisors and college professors, folks who could quote Bible verses from memory and folks who didn't know Genesis from NASCAR. But I'd never been part of a group with anyone like Gloria.

Like banks, families, and businesses, churches have unwritten rules. Unspoken and unpublished, such regulations are simply understood. And practiced—meticulously. One of those rules is "Don't testify against yourself." But in our small group meetings Gloria would talk about former days of drinking herself numb, getting what she called "s***-faced," and dancing on tables in a bar. Another rule is "Don't swear." Imagine an entirely new church where only ten people have known each other longer than four months. While many of us would be visiting with new attendees in our undersized lobby, Gloria might be in the parking lot telling someone, "I don't give a d*** what you think." I never knew if I should stop her or encourage her. A third rule, rigorously practiced by most rookie church attendees, is "If you don't know what they're talking about, fake it." Faced with new information, specifically new Bible information, most people in small groups succumb to the

powerful temptation to pretend, refusing to admit they
don't understand something. Most will remain quiet or
scratch their chin thoughtfully and say, "Hmmmmm, that's
a good question." But after reading a disturbing Bible passage, Gloria would voice what everyone else was thinking:
"What the h*** was *that* about?"

Three months into our new group, Gloria told us she
had just been diagnosed with a fast-acting type of ovarian
cancer. But she also announced that, thanks to our warehouse church, she had strong faith. Despite her doctor's
prognosis to the contrary, she informed us that she was
going to survive this cancer. And for the next ten years she
did survive. She fought that cancer through surgery after
surgery in a seemingly unending process she came to call
her personal weight loss program—"you keep removing
body parts and adding scars." Bravely Gloria battled her illness. Some days were tolerable; most were not. We were all
amazed at her resilience.

Once I asked Gloria, "What do you think about when
you go through the doors into surgery?" Without hesitation she replied, as if it were the most obvious thing in
the world, "Before I go into the hospital, I write Bible
verses on little pieces of paper and then I hold them in my
hands as I go into surgery." I asked, "What sort of verses
do you write out?" She said, "The Lord is my light and my
strength, whom shall I fear?" and "One thing I ask of the
Lord, this is what I seek, to gaze upon the beauty of the
Lord. . . ."

The week after Gloria died I met with her live-in boy-
friend of fifteen years. Years earlier she had informed me,
"I know you want us to get married, but I've got cancer;
what can we *do* anyway?" Like Gloria, he was a long-term

church outsider. Once I saw him driving ahead of me on the same road. I gave him what I intended as a friendly car-horn hello. Not recognizing me and assuming I found his driving objectionable, he stuck his arm out his truck window and gave me a one-fingered salute instantly recognizable to me and to my fellow motorists. Grieving that day in my office he was far more subdued and grateful. "Gloria loved the church. She was always so thankful for the friends she made here." And then he added, "She was a different person after she started to come here." We both knew that Gloria had remained very much the same. Her sarcastic wit, lethal honesty, and zest for life undiminished, she was so very *Gloria*. But, he said, she was also new. She was more patient, more deeply at peace, and confident that Jesus really would walk with her through the valley of the shadow of death. An encounter with the beauty of the Lord had changed her.

The last time Gloria visited my office she had an agenda. First she handed me a letter-sized envelope. When attending church, often wearing glittering jewelry, dazzling wigs, or flamboyant hair wraps she would drop twenty dollars in the offering. Her string of cancer surgeries and long recovery times had kept her away. So inside the envelope was thirty weeks of offerings. In her wonderful gravelly voice and matter-of-fact way she barked, "This is for the church." Then we talked. Our conversation rambled from the "old days" of our church (which was eight years old at the time), to growing up in Michigan, to her recent houseboat trip. But most of all we talked about her funeral, the moment her friends would gather after her death to remember her. "I want you to do the service," she said. Then she fixed her eyes on me and pointed her index finger like a master sergeant commanding an outranked inferior. "And I don't want it to be depressing." "What do you want me to say?" I asked. She answered without hesitation, "I want you to tell them about Jesus. Let them know about him. I want them to see God too."

Weeks later, a dizzying mishmash of Gloria's family members, former drinking buddies, and church friends gathered for her funeral. Many had cleaned her home, done her shopping, and made impromptu Taco Bell trips to satisfy her infrequent but intense after-chemo food cravings. We told Gloria stories. We sang. We laughed. We celebrated her life. I eulogized her with a few escapades, tame compared to the boisterous tales offered by her drinking friends. And then, as ordered, I invited everyone to pray like Gloria, to gaze upon the beauty of the Lord, a beauty burly enough to get a person through repeated cancer surgeries, sneaky enough to surprise the most irreligious person into a full-bodied faith.

Like Simone Weil and like Gloria, "Jack" Lewis was a deeply-rooted doubter before he experienced an unexpected conversion. In fact, his joining the ranks of the faithful was so unexpected that he titled his spiritual biography *Surprised by Joy* (well before he became engaged to a surprising American woman named Joy). Unlike Weil, Lewis's entrance into the Christian faith did not arise from an overpowering, unexplainable mystical experience but through the ordinary routines of late-night walks and discussions with friends. During one such walk Lewis was talking with his friends Hugo Dyson and J. R. R. Tolkien about the true nature of stories, specifically myths. Lewis argued that myths, though beautiful, were only "lies and

therefore worthless, even though breathed through silver."
Tolkien disagreed vigorously. Far from being lies, he said,
they were the best way—sometimes the only way—of
conveying truths that would otherwise remain inexpress-
ible. Because humans have come from God, he argued, the
myths we weave "reflect a splintered fragment of the true
light, of the eternal truth that is with God. Myths may be
misguided, but they steer however shakily toward the true
harbor."[9]

Such late night conversations, lubricated by brilliant minds and often by pints of beer, birthed Lewis's
faith. It grew through regular attendance at the chapel at
Magdalen College in Oxford, where the service of Morning
Prayer read from *The Book of Common Prayer* was largely
unchanged since the sixteenth century. In this way Lewis
"went through the whole of the Psalms many times, he
certainly knew the entire Psalter by heart."[10] Taken in and
memorized, the stately Elizabethan tones of the Psalter
profoundly shaped Lewis's faith and his writings.

Late in life, long after publishing his famous Chronicles
of Narnia series for children and more than a dozen works
of theology, the Oxford University professor served on
an Anglican Church committee to revise the Psalter. The
committee's aim was to adapt the collection of psalms in
the *Book of Common Prayer*, translations that were taken
wholly from Miles Coverdale's first English translation of
the Bible, completed in 1535. A work of profound beauty,
deeply poetic, Coverdale's translation is filled with unforgettable lines of prayer still used in Anglican circles half
a millennium after his initial writing. Lewis, a creative
author, former atheist, and tradition-bound church-goer,
agreed to serve on the committee, largely "in order to dis-

courage revisions, since he thought the Miles Coverdale version that had been in use for four hundred years more than adequate," an opinion shared by T. S. Eliot, another member of the committee.[11]

Writing on Psalm 27, this skeptic-turned-believer confessed, "The most valuable thing the psalms do for me is to express the delight in God which made David dance." When compared to the dutiful "church-going" and "laborious 'saying our prayers'" to which Christians are sometimes reduced, Psalm 27 "stands out as something astonishingly robust, virile, and spontaneous; something we may regard with an innocent envy and may hope to be infected by as we read."[12] For the psalmist of Psalm 27, engaging in the most ordinary act of worship is to "gaze on the beauty of the Lord."

Lewis particularly liked this psalm because it encouraged mirth in worship, something he found singularly lacking in Anglicans, with their "terrible concern about good taste." Good taste, he said, is not the point of Psalm 27. Instead the psalmist seeks "an experience fully God-centred, asking of God no gift more urgently than His presence, the gift of Himself, joyous to the highest degree, and unmistakably real."[13] Lewis stressed our need to develop an appetite for the "joy and delight in God which meet us in the psalms," the living center of faith.

Spurgeon aimed for the same experience of deep joy sought by Jack Lewis. Sounding like the veteran minister and master encourager he was, he implored, "Think of it, dear reader! Better far—behold it by faith! What a sight will that be when every faithful follower of Jesus shall behold 'the King in his beauty!' Oh, for that infinitely blessed vision!" In his commentary on Psalm 27 he writes:

To behold the beauty of the Lord. An exercise both for earthly and heavenly worshippers. We must not enter the assemblies of the saints in order to see and be seen, or merely to hear the minister; we must repair to the gatherings of the righteous, intent upon the gracious object of learning more of the loving Father, more of the glorified Jesus, more of the mysterious Spirit, in order that we may the more lovingly admire, and the more reverently adore our glorious God.[14]

The beauty of the Lord is the one thing desirable that Christ speaks of in the gospel. It's the one thing, says Spurgeon, "which, if a Christian had, he needs desire no more." For those who love God, it "is enough even to satisfy us, the fruition of God, and the beholding of him . . . to have correspondence and fellowship and communion with him there."

Generations of spiritual insiders and outsiders have found themselves changed or renewed by praying this psalm. As Weil writes, beauty requires us to "give up our imaginary position as the center."[15] Inspired by Weil's comment, Elaine Scarry argues that in the presence of beauty we are transformed. "It is not," she says, "that we cease to stand at the center of the world, for we never stood there. It is that we cease to stand even at the center of our own world. We willingly cede our ground to the thing that stands before us."[16]

An uninitiated person might assume that gazing "on the beauty of the Lord" is a kind of self-focused spiritual narcissism, a way to make all our prayer about us. But biblical

commentator Walter Brueggemann says that the actual
result of experiencing beauty is a new, powerful stirring to
work for justice. In Psalm 27 the writer's feeling of safety
in the Lord leads to praise and sacrifice.[17] That's why it's
no surprise that later on in life, after her rapturous experience of Christ's presence through the lines of Herbert's
poem, Weil moved to Harlem to live among the poor.
Subsequently she moved to London, where she joined the
French Resistance. Even when diagnosed with tuberculosis
she refused special treatment, limiting her food intake to
the rations available to residents in occupied France.

Like Weil and Spurgeon, Martin Luther King Jr.'s
prayer life fueled his solidarity with ordinary, suffering
people. Born into middle class surroundings and inheriting
religion from his preacher father, King seemed an unlikely
leader for the civil rights movement. Organizers of what
became the famous bus boycott chose him simply because
he was new to Montgomery, and city fathers had not yet
had time to intimidate him. Now we know they chose better than they could have imagined.

Dr. King's stirring words inspired his followers with
the courage to confront the grim circumstances of their
lives. In September 1955, preaching in Montgomery's
Dexter Avenue Baptist Church, King pointed his Alabama
parishioners to Psalm 27: "Life constantly presents us with
circumstances which are beyond our control . . . we are
continually confronted with circumstances which we did
not have the freedom to choose, but with which we are
forced to deal." At birth, he reminded congregants, African
Americans are "automatically thrust into a caste system"
they didn't select. Other people, through no fault of their
own, are forced to live with an unwelcome and dreaded

disease. In such intolerable circumstances, he said, one of the great temptations of life is to become "inward thinking." Passionately and confidently he urged his congregation to choose a different path,

> Whenever a man looks merely at his circumstances he ends up in despair, disillusionment and cynicism. . . . The great burden of life then, is to master the art of looking beyond one's circumstances. Ultimately the test of a man's life is how he responds to his circumstances. One day the Psalmist was meditating on his circumstances. . . . He cried out, "I had fainted unless I believed to see the goodness of the Lord. . . ."[18]

That is, the psalmist would have given in to despair unless he had the courage to look beyond his circumstances. King concluded, "It is necessary to look beyond our circumstances to something fixed . . . knowing God's beautiful goodness will ultimately win over every state of evil."

On February 1, 1965, sensing that their movement had made some local progress but was stalled far short of the justice they sought, King led a march of three hundred people. He and his key aide, Ralph Abernathy, were arrested and placed in a steamy, ninety-foot holding cell. In no shape to give a speech, King proposed a Quaker style meeting: any prisoner could lead a song, give a speech, or pray. Abernathy opened that jail-house meeting reading from Psalm 27, his personal favorite. "The LORD is my light and my salvation, whom shall I fear?" His opening words released a litany of prayer and song that continued well into the night.[19]

The civil rights movement continued to grow, at times with help from unlikely places. Rabbi Abraham Joshua Heschel was born in Warsaw and grew up in Berlin. He was raised in a strictly religious Hasidic community; both his father and grandfather were well-known orthodox rabbis. Escaping the Nazis, Heschel immigrated to the United States in 1940. In one sense Heschel was like Spurgeon, the prototypical religious insider. But in another he was very much like Weil—an unlikely combination of introversion, fire, and revolutionary spirit. He pushed for authentic Jewish prayer, denouncing the habit of "praying by proxy"—that is, letting the rabbi and cantor do the work. He asked provocative questions like "Has the synagogue become the graveyard where prayer is buried?"[20] After first meeting King in January of 1963, Heschel joined the civil rights movement, lecturing and demonstrating on its behalf.

In March 1965 Heschel joined King and Abernathy on the third Selma protest march. Two weeks earlier Alabama state police had confronted marchers with clubs and tear gas. The setting for this new march was festive; many wore Hawaiian leis, a gift from one of the participants. But fears remained—fears for Heschel's safety, as well as that of the other leaders, as onlookers voiced racial hatred and bitter anti-Semitism.

Before the march King led a Sunday worship service. Two hundred people packed Brown's chapel, where many had spent the night, and three thousand more were gathered outside, waiting. King began the service by welcoming out-of-state participants. Then Heschel read from Psalm 27: "The LORD is my light and my salvation, whom shall I fear? The LORD is the strength of my life, of whom shall I be afraid?" King followed with a sermon about the Israelites who wandered in the desert after the exodus from Egypt.

Before the march began, Heschel insisted on walking in the front row. He knew that newsreels featuring his generous beard and yarmulke-crowned white hair would confirm the popular image of a rabbi. So he marched in front, joining hands with Ralf Bunche, former undersecretary of the United Nations, King, Abernathy, and others. As they marched slowly through Selma, hostile onlookers cursed and jeered. Frowning old women sat in rocking chairs on their front porches, displaying homemade banners with messages like "Koons, Kikes and Niggers Go Home!" Police officers drove by in squad cars, filming participants. Many marchers found the National Guard's presence more fear-inducing and threatening than protective.[21]

For Heschel the march was not simply about politics. It was primarily an act of faith, a revival of the age-long, prophetic push for social justice, a renewal of the idea that compassion for suffering people defines a truly religious person. Later his daughter Susannah wrote, "He saw [the march] as a revival of prophetic Judaism's political activism and also of the traditions of Hasidism, a Jewish pietistic revival movement that arose in the late eighteenth century, according to which walking could be a spiritual experience."[22]

Weil remained the outsider, wrestling with the church's tendency to reject, divide, and call people and other traditions unfit. How could the church represent Jesus, the incarnated Jew? She believed such tyranny called for confrontation. Only forsaking its hideous history of exclusion and self-righteousness would enable the church to live out its potential to represent Jesus. In a letter to a French priest written in 1942, Weil described her struggle to reconcile the unsightly history of the church with the beauty of Christ:

> I have been thinking about these things for years with all the intensity of love and attention of which I am capable. . . . In proportion as it grows, the bonds which attach me to the Catholic faith become ever stronger and stronger, ever more deeply rooted in the heart and intelligence. But at the same time the thoughts which separate me from the Church also gain force and clarity. If these thoughts are really incompatible with membership of the Church, then there is no hope that I may ever take part in the sacraments. If such is the case, I do not see how I can avoid the conclusion that my vocation is to be a Christian outside the Church.[23]

Some biographers say that Weil, after years of agonizing, was baptized into the church. Others are less certain. In either case, Weil had become, to some real extent, an insider. Praying the ageless book of prayer, fixed on the "beauty of the Lord," her never-ending protests joined the marches of Heschel, the preaching of Spurgeon and King, the testimony of Lewis, the life of Gloria, the music of Bernstein—all, in a way, prayers. Prayers of people who had been reoriented and transformed by "the beauty of the Lord."

BALLAST FOR GENERATIONS

PSALM 42

"God behaves in the psalms in ways he is not allowed to behave in systematic theology."[1]

—Sebastian Moore

As the deer pants for streams of water, so my soul pants for you, my
    God.
My soul thirsts for God, for the living God.
When can I go and meet with God?
My tears have been my food day and night,
while people say to me all day long, "Where is your God?"
These things I remember as I pour out my soul:
how I used to go to the house of God under the protection of the
    Mighty One
with shouts of joy and praise among the festive throng.
Why, my soul, are you downcast? Why so disturbed within me?

Put your hope in God,
for I will yet praise him, my Savior and my God.

—Psalm 42:1-5

Rags were piled at the foot of his bed. Patients, the doctor had warned, often vomited blood when stomach cancer finally conquered them. All day there had been an odd and terrible winter thunderstorm. Friends visited anyway, gathering around his bedside as they had for days, singing one psalm after another. Verse after verse, their unhurried melodies rose; the metrical psalms they had learned as children in another land steeling their faith during this trying hour. My aunt, a young mom at the time, remembers cleaning the house as the tunes ascended to the second story where she dusted, scrubbed, and worried.

That evening, on Christmas Eve, the family was seated in a circle around their beloved dying father. He lay in his hospital bed, centered in the living room like an unwelcome altar. He held hands with his wife. Married more than thirty years, she was, like him, a sturdy immigrant, banking that their hard work and firm faith would build a better life for their family in this new country. He asked, "Could I have a cup of coffee?" His request shocked her—it had been so long since he had asked for such a thing. When she gladly went to get it, she found him in the bathroom putting on his long johns. He hadn't gotten up in a long time, and now he was rummaging about the house. Lying down again on the hospital bed, he was quiet for a while. Then he raised his body slightly, tilting his head as if listening. Abruptly he sat straight up in bed. "Listen," he said, "I hear them singing." He softly smiled, leaned back on the bed, shut his eyes, and was gone. His wife said, "Goodnight here and good morning there." His daughters cried and his square-shouldered son fainted next to the bed. It was just after midnight, Christmas morning.

Six months earlier John had been visiting a beach town with his children and grandchildren. After a leisurely day, he was enjoying a hot beef sandwich when suddenly he didn't feel well. The family sped home as quickly as two toddler grandchildren allowed. The next day he called a nurse friend for advice. "Call the doctor," she prescribed. When the doctor arrived at the house for the examination, he ordered John to go immediately to the hospital. There they pronounced his sentence: six months. He was full of cancer. On hearing the news, his son-in-law began to cry. John said, "You must be feeling bad, thinking of how you lost your own dad already." "No," he replied, "I love you too, Pa."

Like many immigrants, John did manual labor, eventually working twenty-five years for the city maintenance division. Wielding a jackhammer, he replaced city sidewalks or built retaining walls. His coworkers loved his dependability; it empowered their sloth. They would give him a cigarette and then retreat into the shade for a drink, leaving him to start a project, or finish it, or both. He didn't mind so much. He had a job and a good life. His grandkids visited often. He played the accordion. Every week his wife bought two cigars with the Saturday groceries; those evenings dear friends would visit and they'd talk freely in the smoke-clouded living room.

At his winter funeral the congregation sang the same psalms they had sung around his bedside: Psalm 23, Psalm 16, and Psalm 42—"As the deer pants for streams of water, so my soul pants for you, my God." The psalms gave his grieving family and their fellow churchgoers strength to face their fears, to endure the trials of a new land, even to grieve a death on Christmas morning. I don't remember the funeral—two-year-old grandsons are not considered appropriate mourners. But I do remember that at some point each Christmas of my childhood, a wistful look would come over my mother's face and she would say, "This is the day my dad died."

Four years earlier, before my parents were engaged, before my dad was twenty years old, his father was diagnosed with lung cancer. A spot welder, he built industrial-size fans, welding parts into place. Working in the era before safety masks and OSHA regulations, he brought his work home with him each night in the fine-particle toxins that filled his lungs. On the outside his life was fine. His trade paid a decent wage, helping him buy modest comforts, even as, unknown to him or his family, ultraviolet light and heat were mixing with toxic contaminants and wreaking havoc in his lungs. His health deflated as quickly as a lacerated balloon. His teeth rotted in his mouth; he looked as if death were swallowing him. Hoping to spare him misery, his wife never told him of the doctor's fatal diagnosis. He discovered the truth about his cancer when his brother-in-law spilled the secret. His children kept vigil each night, offering small comforts, wetting his lips with moist clothes and relating details of the day. A few weeks after his diagnosis, he slipped into a coma and was gone.

I never met this grandfather. He lived when audio and video recordings were a luxury of the wealthy. He was an ordinary working man. A few photographs help me picture him, and a few books he left behind. I have the lunch box he carried each day to his welding job. He scratched his initials on the side: KA. How could he have known they would be mine? As I grow older, his legacy appears from the mist of memories not my own, from puzzle pieces in the faces of his brothers, my dad's uncles, and in the quiet ways of my own father. My dad remembers family devotions at supper time, his father far too shy to pray aloud, even among his own children. Each evening, without expression and without fail, he would read fifteen or twenty verses from the Bible. Then he prayed silently, bowing his head. When finished, he made a slight sniffle. On cue my dad and his two younger sisters then spoke the rote mealtime prayers of their childhood.

One of my own memories further sharpens his picture. The Sundays our family visited Grandma for dinner, she would read the same Bible passage: Psalm 139. Every time. As a child I didn't give it any thought. She fixed the same prepackaged meat, the same vegetables, and the same dessert. At restaurants she gave the waitress the same order, and if they botched the order, she gave them the same glaring reprimand. Why shouldn't she read the same Bible text? When I finally asked why, she said, "It was Grandpa's favorite." Why might a strongly introverted person treasure a psalm that begins, "O LORD, you have searched me and you know me"?

He loved life. He hunted and fished with passion. Many of his Saturdays he spent with the local volunteer fire department. Each buck, each bass, each doused fire brought him delight. He was a simple man with the deep and noble simplicity I see in my father and hope one day to see in the mirror. Praying felt awkward to him; he was ill at ease, self-conscious even in the presence of his young children, but he prayed anyway. That he owed them. Style wasn't important to him. Neither was creativity. But he aimed to bury within his family an intangible fortune to carry them into the future.

Both of my grandfathers gave me a treasure. And like many family treasures, for the longest time I didn't know I had it.

———————————

Unlike my paternal grandfather, Ben Patterson lives his faith with gregarious freedom. A creative, articulate, fervent Christian pastor, he has spent much of his life working on college campuses. When you meet him, you understand why. His eyes, overflowing with life, twinkle above his Santa-like beard. His smile is contagious. When he speaks, students readily listen. Now in his sixties, you can't imagine him ever being out of vogue. College students continue to be drawn to his winsome, witty ways.

When he was a college sophomore, Ben and some friends decided one day that they should spend two hours praying for the spiritually detached high school students in their charge. These students were part of their ministry group, and the leaders were unsure what else to do with them. So they decided to pray. They gathered at church that night in the only room available, a janitor's closet that smelled like industrial strength detergent. With their piety in high gear, they knelt in that closet and poured out their prayer. "We prayed every which way we knew: we praised God and confessed our sins and lifted up the names of all the students we could think of. Then we praised and confessed and interceded some more. When I looked at my watch, just fifteen minutes had passed! The next hour and 45 minutes of prayer were the longest and slowest I had ever experienced."[2]

Recalling that day decades later, Patterson says he came to pour out his heart to God and discovered there wasn't much to pour out. Only years later did he understand what went wrong that night. The trouble in the janitor's closet wasn't their youthful zeal, or the smelly setting, or a lack of subject. No, the problem was that his prayer was stuffed with *himself*. It brimmed over with "me and Jesus," not "we and Jesus."

Ben didn't grow up in the church. He became a follower of Jesus at ten years old. At his family meals, no one read Bible passages or signaled the end to silent prayers with a subtle sniffle. Ben assumed that prayer demanded his own words—it was really about him. He read the psalms, he says, but it wasn't until he discovered Eugene Peterson's phrase "No Christian is an only child" that the psalms made any sense. Now Ben prays the psalms as part of the community of faith. Even when he is praying solo, he imagines himself praying among a huge gathering of fellow believers. That treasure is one some people inherit from their grandparents.

Andras Visky is one of those people. Ask him about his first memory and he'll tell you that it is of prison. Along with his six siblings and his mother, Julia, Andras was sentenced to a Romanian labor camp at the Danube Delta. In prison, he says, grass was often their meal, and his mother tried to prepare it well. Forty years later he has an official state document from those childhood prison days stating that he was a dangerous criminal of the state. He was two years old.

After the heady, short-lived days of the 1956 Hungarian Revolution, Andras's father, Ferenc, was sentenced to twenty-two years in a notorious communist prison. His offense as a pastor in the Hungarian Reformed Church was "crimes against the state." In his memoir, *The Foolishness of God*, he says that the madness of the world, including that of the then Soviet system, can only be dispelled by the foolishness of God. Even in times of great darkness he sensed God's presence, bringing comfort in the darkness, even laughter. In prison, Andras says, he learned to laugh. And in his laughter he held on to God, wrestling with him for a sign.

Ferenc had learned the psalms as a young child, falling asleep each night in his parents' bedroom with the florescent words of Psalm 73:28 glowing into his memory from a picture on the wall: "But as for me, it is good to be near God. I have made the sovereign Lord my refuge." When they married in 1947, Ferenc and Julia Visky chose the words of Psalm 115:1 as their guide: "Not to us, LORD, not to us but to your name be the glory, because of your love and faithfulness." That love, they say, upheld them through the six hard years of Ferenc's imprisonment, Julia's detention with the children, and ordinary days of betrayal and interrogation—the routine anguish integral to Romanian communism.[3]

Andras now works as a playwright and the resident dramaturge of the Hungarian State Theatre. Having grown up in a Gulag, his plays return again and again to what it means to be a detainee and to the puzzle of being set free. Reflecting on his days as a child prisoner, he remembers singing psalms every day, especially at meal times, a tradition in the Hungarian Reformed Church. As a parent, he carries on the tradition of singing at meals and other special events. His teenage daughter's favorite, he says, is Psalm 24.

Retired Romanian musicologist Almasi Istvan reflects on this musical heritage stretching back to the days of the Genevan Psalter's completion in 1569: "You may be absolutely certain that the singing of the psalms did help preserve faith during the Communist era!" Istvan is convinced that the beauty and muscle of sung psalms can capture the next generation. "Music has the power to capture and transform in a way that no other medium can, but the teaching of the psalms to the young depends on the teacher's love for the psalms and the ability to lead the children to Christ," he says.[4]

Unlike the Viskys, Kathleen Norris ditched the religious tradition of her parents and grandparents. Escaping to New York, she obtained work as an arts administrator at the Academy of American Poets, published her first book of poetry, and married fellow poet David Dwyer. For twenty years they lived in the most fashionable, urbane, fast-paced city in the world. Then, surprising everyone, even themselves, they moved back to the town of her childhood. Back to the farm home of her grandparents. Back to Lemmon, South Dakota. Most surprising of all, she found herself going back to the unfashionable, unsophisticated, plodding church of her childhood.

These backward moves came, she says, after she began to realize that her writing was in essence a religious quest. In one way, going back helped her remember what she hated about church, what she had sought to escape by leaving. Growing up, church meant two things: singing and dressing up. The singing she loved, especially as a young child. But when she began to navigate the dizzying maze of female adolescence, dressing up for church became repulsive, a symbol that church was profoundly disconnected from her true self's tangle of adolescent doubts and emotions:

I have lately realized that what went wrong for me in my Christian upbringing is centered in the belief that one had to be dressed up, both outwardly and inwardly, to meet God, the insidious notion that I need to be a firm and even cheerful believer before I dare show my face in "His" church." Such a God was of little use to me in adolescence, and like many women of my generation I simply stopped going to church when I could no longer be "good," which for girls especially meant not breaking rules, not giving voice to anger or resentment, and not complaining.[5]

So she did what any self-respecting young woman would do. She left. Until she came back. Her journey took her further back even than the faith of her grandparents, all the way back to the Benedictines, a monastic order begun in 529. Norris jokes that her prairie town was so isolated that she needed to visit a monastery for excitement. She began visiting the monks first for short monthly retreats and then for lengthy stays. She enjoyed their prayers, their library, their stimulating conversation, and their generous hospitality. Eventually she took vows as an oblate in their Benedictine order.

But at the time she didn't feel ready to formally tie herself to their community. How can a person ever be ready to join an ancient order, to commit to a group of robed monks, to make vows? she wondered. On the edge of her promise, standing in the chapel, she paused, working to sort out her muddled thoughts, the tangle of doubts she'd carried inside since college days. Her oblate director, the monk who had guided her through the workings of the

Benedictine Rule, a study typically lasting a year that she had managed to drag into three, waited patiently for her to sort out her muddle. Finally she told him, "I can't imagine why God would want me, of all people, as an offering. But if God is foolish enough to take me as I am, I guess I'd better do it." The monk smiled and nodded. "You're ready," he said.[6] Whether in Lemmon, South Dakota, in a Benedictine monastery, or in suburban California, thoughtful people, it seems, enter or reenter the family of faith with a mix of joy and misgiving.

During a nine-month stay at the monastery Norris experienced the psalms, chanted seven times a day, in a new way. She learned that "when you go to church several times a day, every day, there is no way you can 'do it right.'" To her surprise, she discovered that the psalms "do not deny your true feelings but allow you to reflect on them, right in front of God and everyone."[7] Tangled up in church expectations and our own, we often toil toward holiness, imagining we must grab the holy by ditching our humanity. But the psalms offer a spirituality rooted in our humanity, a spirituality that is ruthlessly honest about our inadequacy. A Benedictine sister told Norris what it was like to pray the psalms aloud. "At the bedside of her dying mother, who was in a coma, she discovered 'how perfectly the psalms reflected my own inner chaos: my fear of losing her, or of not losing her and seeing her suffer more, of saying goodbye, of being motherless.' She found that the closing lines of Psalm 16—"You will show me the path of life /the fullness of joy in your presence'—consoled her."[8]

Benedictines take three main vows: stability, obedience, and *conversatio,* continual conversion. In the vow of stability an oblate promises lifelong fidelity to God and to his or her community. Obedience is a vow to listen, a decision to act in responsive love to God's voice, whether it comes through prayer, the Rule of Saint Benedict, the Bible, or members of the community. *Conversatio* commits one to embrace all of life as a path to holiness and conversion; it's a "conversion of life." Norris says it means, in part, "that you commit yourself to being changed by the words of the psalms, allowing them to work on you, and sometimes to work you over."[9] Sometimes what they work out of us is our well-learned pattern of idolizing ourselves.

Trained as narcissists, we assume, like Ben Patterson, that even our prayer life is fundamentally about us. But praying psalms in community teaches us to lament even when we are in a good mood. We learn to give thanks even when we feel grim. The prayers of the community roll on with us, or without us. Norris puts it this way, "The liturgy that Benedictines have been experimenting with for 1,500-plus years taught me the value of tradition; I came to see that the psalms are holy in part because they are so well used. If so many generations had found solace here, might I also? The holiness of the psalms came to seem like that of a stone that has been held in the palm by countless ancestors. . . ."[10]

In a surprising twist, praying the psalms in community makes them more truly personal. Freed from the confining tyranny and limits of our own individual experience, they become more deeply our own. Singing the psalms as part of an ageless tradition, our vision for the world, and a clear sense of our place in it, continues to grow.

———————————

Norris's writings have often been compared to those of Thomas Merton, another author turned Benedictine

who found peace in an abbey. When his best-selling autobiography, *The Seven Storey Mountain*, was released in 1948,
hundreds of disillusioned students and World War II veterans flocked to monasteries across the United States. In
the abbey, a place of deep quiet, Merton wrote more than
seventy books of poems, spirituality, and social justice.
Ironically, this prolific writing made the solitude for which
he yearned more elusive. Craving the first-hand knowledge
and experience of God available in the psalms, Merton
chose to live as a Trappist monk, where he and his fellow
monks chanted the entire Psalter every two weeks in the
seven daily offices. His spiritual quest didn't end when he
entered the cloister walls, Merton tells us, but continued
throughout his monastic life.

Much of Merton's writing points his readers to the
treasure of the psalms, the ancient school for the soul. "In
the Psalms," he wrote, "we drink divine praise at its pure
and stainless source, in all its primitive sincerity and per-
fection."[11] Merton described the psalms as nourishment for
the inner life; they formed the substance of the community's meditation and that of his own personal prayer. He
called them the "Liturgy of Heaven." Chanting the psalms,
he said, we voice a love song on earth in preparation for
heaven.[12]

Those who enter the psalms find a surprising depth.
In them God gives us himself, as though in a sacrament.
When we sing the psalms together, we sing of our knowledge of God, our union with him.[13] This may not happen
immediately. At first their language may seem unfamiliar,
their vocabulary as foreign as a Chinese subway map, but
praying them regularly, one comes at last "to live them and

experience them as if they were his own songs, his own prayers."[14]

Merton says we can divide people of prayer into three groups according to their attitudes about the psalms. The first group admits in theory that the psalms are wonderful helps in prayer, but they never get around to actually praying them. Cornered into reciting psalms, they sound like a junior high English class reluctantly mumbling Shakespeare's *Romeo and Juliet*. The second group has a strong conviction about the value of the psalms, and some even argue belligerently for their use in worship or individual prayer—but their zeal is external. It's good enough for them that the church of all times and places has valued the psalms, and what was good enough then is good enough now. The third group, a small minority, knows *by experience* that the psalms are perfect prayer, that Christ himself prays them in us. They have, in a real sense, lived the meaning of the psalms in their own lives.[15]

While writing this chapter, I spent a day in a monastic spin-off from Merton's home abbey in Kentucky. The Abbey of New Clairvaux rests on 500 flat, beautiful acres of California orchard. It began in the 1950s from the overflow of monastic entrants inspired by Merton's writings. At breakfast I met a twenty-something man named Edward. Raised both in Oakland and Quebec, Edward appeared endlessly fascinating. He was, I soon discovered, an artist, playwright, philosopher, and most willing conversationalist—even on silent retreat. Until arriving at the monastery the previous evening, Edward had been homeless, sleeping in his car, looking for work, and fighting with his girlfriend, with whom he had been sharing his automotive home. Exhausted from endless arguments, searching for something more, he finally took the advice of a Sacramento priest to visit the Trappists. At least there, said the priest, he would have food to eat and a bed to sleep in. And so, desperate for peace and a place to belong, Edward went.

We met in the guest dining hall, a small converted farm cottage built in the early 1900s. Edward was carrying a sketchpad, writing whatever struck his fancy, looking for a way to use his talents. Despite his recent wanderings, he appeared so confident, so dynamic and full of verve that I half-expected him, after a couple of weeks on site, to rechoreograph fifteen hundred years of ancient monastic chants into something with a more urban flair. He was happiest, he told me, when digging in the soil or playing wooden instruments like the violin or flute, or, I quickly surmised during our first conversation, *talking*.

He pulled up a chair to join me at the table where I had been silently eating my breakfast. The more he talked, the more I pictured him as a young Thomas Merton—intense, brilliant, restless, with a bias toward action, someone who might fully live in the world by withdrawing from it. I told him Merton's story, and then I suggested that he might find his autobiography most interesting and that he was likely to find a copy in the monastic library a few steps away. Edward's eyes lit up and he burst into a broad smile. "A *suggestion?*" he said. "The sort of *suggestion* I'd be a fool not to take?"

Early in the conversation, like a detective inspecting a crime scene, Edward had discovered my occupation and was on to my pastor ways. Still I wondered if he might be a living example of Psalm 42. Might all his philosophical musings, dramatic impulses, and relational turbulence be evidence of the psalmist's longing: "As the deer pants for streams of water, so my soul pants for you, my God"? As we parted company I wondered about Edward's prospects at the monastery, that psalm-saturated place. Might another well-trained narcissist finally find his true family, a place to belong? Might he find the psalms merely personal, or truly personal?

Merton described Psalm 42 as "the joy of a soul that knows how to hope in the hour that would otherwise seem nothing but despair."[16] Norris points out that the psalm "moves the way our emotions do, in fits and starts: 'Why are you cast down my soul? Why groan within me?' . . . But its true theme is a desire for the holy that, whatever form it takes, seems to be a part of the human condition, a desire easily forgotten in the pull and tug of daily life, where groans of despair can predominate." She goes on to quote a Benedictine sister who wrote to her: "Some winters ago, when ice covered all the lands surrounding our priory, deer came close in search of food. We had difficulty keeping them from eating our trees and even the shrubs in our cemetery." Having been at the convent for many years, says Norris, this sister had known most of the women buried there. One morning she woke to find that "each deer had selected a particular tombstone to lie behind, oblivious to us watching from the priory windows. The longing for God expressed at the beginning of Psalm 42, 'Like the deer that yearns for running streams, so my soul is yearning for you, My God' has stayed with me ever since."[17]

———————

A few months ago a hard-working and dedicated fellow pastor with twenty-five years' experience told me what it was like to visit his twenty-two-year-old daughter as she lay in a hospital. For months she had been suffering mysterious seizures. My friend and his wife would hear what first sounded like someone thumping on her bedroom wall. Then they'd find their daughter in convulsions, shaking and helpless, unable to speak. Doctors could prescribe medication, but they admitted that they had little idea of what was happening in her body.

Only days before visiting his daughter, this pastor had conducted the funeral of a close friend's son. Athletic and strong, bursting with patriotism and valor, the friend's son had joined the Army, hoping for frontline duty in Iraq, determined to make a difference in the world. He returned to his country in a body bag. Walking into his daughter's hospital room that summer day, with this funeral fresh in his mind, my pastor friend thought, "I don't know if I believe or not." In the hospital room next to his daughter's, a man kept vigil at the bedside of his dying wife. Ordinarily my pastor friend would stop in and speak a word of kindness to this man, embodying the compassion of Jesus. But that day he didn't have anything to say. He doubted that he had anything to offer. With his own spiritual GPS on the fritz, my friend was too lost himself to offer spiritual guidance.

Most of us resonate with loss. Our life is stuffed with losing. We lose our youth, we lose our hair, we lose our figure, we lose our strength or the hope of ever gaining it back. Some of us lose our hearing or our sight, even our memory. Belonging to a church or family often connects us to losing. A prolonged argument wears away our hope for an idyllic family life. A heated dispute splits a church into factions. A young daughter lies in a hospital bed while the cause of her seizures hides undiagnosed.

Last month my son's girlfriend visited our home for the first time. These college sweethearts hadn't seen each other for months. Starving for time together after a summer apart and before the next semester's studies would keep them a continent apart, they often slipped away for quiet walks and hallway conversations. One moment they were deep into kibitzing with the family around our kitchen table, the next they'd vanish for a multi-hour stroll. Most of our extended family had yet to meet our son's significant other. We imagined that she would join our backyard barbeques, evening strolls, and heart-to-heart chats. But together they often became a disappearing act. Don't get me wrong. We like her. Our whole family *really* likes her. She's bright, thoughtful, and kind and makes our son's face turn what his roommate describes as "all smiley." They are so happy in each other's company. But inside I felt loss. I was watching him slip away. Veteran fathers had warned me about the day an unwieldy gorilla, disguised as an adolescent boy, would knock on our front door asking to take our daughter on a date. But no one had warned us about the lovely princess who would dance into our home and waltz off with our son.

Fellow churchgoers would smile at my feelings. When we began our church, young, mostly married adults filled our seats. Our nursery overflowed. Couples scrambled to find time for a walk or a date. Like their pastor, our church was young and hip. That was twenty years ago. Now those same couples walk past empty bedrooms, their children off to college or starting a new life in another city. Any parent is happy when their child finds the joy of true love, even if it's the sort of happiness that mingles with the sense of loss that comes with passing time. But how do we prepare for, how do we stay resilient in a lifetime of loss?

My grandma lived for eighteen years after her husband's death early on Christmas morning. She lived in the house he'd built, the house in which he died. The neighborhood around her changed. Fellow immigrants from her homeland moved to outlying areas, and folks of a different ethnicity moved across the street and next door. It was another sort of loss, but one that came with its own opportunity, and so she stayed. She never learned to drive a car, never read a work of great literature, never bought herself a television set—though her daughter gave her one. But she made a lemon meringue pie to die for, laughed her way through endless games of dominoes with her grandchildren, mowed her own lawn, and kept the house that John built sparkling clean. When my two brothers and I had sleepovers at her house during our elementary school years, we'd tiptoe down the stairs each morning to find her sitting by a window, singing softly, her psalm book open on her lap. At the time, of course, most of my grade school mind focused on the promising possibility of Grandma's breakfast. But as I think about it now, the faraway look on her face gave me the sense that she wasn't singing alone.

Grandma baked cookies the night before she died, leaving them neatly packaged in the kitchen, as if she wanted to fill us with baked goods one more time. Her prune juice and aspirin sat undisturbed on the Formica kitchen table. Just like that, in the middle of the night, alone in her chair, she was gone.

She was the last of her generation, following all her brothers and sisters. At her funeral our family sat together mourning our loss. We found one of her friends, someone from her generation, from her first country, to sing one of her favorite psalms, Psalm 42, in her native Dutch.

't Hijgend hert, der jacht ontkomen,	As a deer in want of water,
Schreeuwt niet sterker naar 't genot	so I long for you, O LORD.
Van de frisse waterstromen,	All my heart and being falter,
Dan mijn ziel verlangt naar God.	thirsting for your living word.
Ja, mijn ziel dorst naar den Heer';	When shall I behold your face?
God des levens, ach, wanneer	When shall I receive your grace?
Zal ik naadren voor Uw ogen,	When shall I, your praises voicing,
In Uw huis Uw Naam verhogen?	Come before you with rejoicing?

That's the sort of song that can get you and your family through loss. Even when it happens on Christmas Day.

TWO FUNERALS
AND A CLAVICLE

PSALM 103

Fatherlike he tends and spares us;
well our feeble frame he knows.
In his hands he gently bears us,
rescues us from all our foes.

—Henry F. Lyte, 1834

As for mortals, their days are like grass;
they flourish like a flower of the field;
for the wind passes over it, and it is gone,
and its place knows it no more.

—Psalm 103:15-16, NRSV

I conducted two funerals one sunny summer Saturday. Both were for people I hadn't met. The truth is, most of the funerals I conduct are for people I haven't met. The great majority of people in our neighborhood have no connection to a religious organization of any kind. Maybe that's because folks who've avoided church most of their lives find little reason to attend after they retire. Or maybe it's simply because few congregations in our up-and-coming suburb have permanent facilities, and we're one of a limited number of options. Often the phone call comes from someone who does attend our church: "My dad wasn't really religious, and you don't need to pretend he was. But would you conduct the funeral for the family?" Other grievers find us by flipping through the yellow pages or driving past our building. "Can you help with a funeral for my aunt?" One family asked us to conduct a funeral with dolphin-themed photos of the deceased and ocean music. A grieving husband, who hadn't been to church since the end of World War II, found us online. I say yes as often as I can.

Author and preacher Neal Plantinga may be the most articulate person I know. He tells seminary students, "At a funeral the gospel plays like a well-tuned Stradivarius violin." Of course, there are other times when the gospel sounds as misplaced as a Wal-Mart guitar on an Albinoni concerto. Or maybe it's the person playing.

I'm often moved to tears by the photos of the deceased that are displayed at funerals, even when I've never met the person. Families display photos of their loved one flourishing. You won't find photos highlighting her agony after a recent surgery or the grim week she spent in a coma connected to a respirator. Instead they show her skiing on an

Alpine lake, or surrounded by family at a wooded park, or toasting the sunset at a beachside restaurant. They show their missing loved one leaning against a classic car he recently rebuilt or smiling after receiving a master's degree.

The first funeral that sunny suburban Saturday was for a woman born in dustbowl Texas. Her two daughters found our church on the Internet. Would I recount their mother's life at the service? In the days leading to her funeral, her daughters and I chatted about their remarkable mother via email and phone messages.

Born in 1935, the decade of black dusters and unemployment, her dad supplemented the family income with a business of his own, moonshine. Reveling in the Texas flatlands, he hated hills and trees; he and his friends wanted to see a long distance. They needed to know exactly who was driving toward their ranch. She was barely five years old when her eleven-year-old sister died of pneumonia. Grief counseling wasn't big in dustbowl Texas, and the family coped by relocating to California, the promised land. There her dad found a welding job in the shipyards and bought a new home in Los Angeles, where they settled. At fourteen she fell madly in love with a twenty-year-old Finnish man from Michigan. He worked in a flower shop when they met but soon joined the Coast Guard. As her daughters said, "Who can resist a man in uniform?" Married at sixteen before she finished high school, she waved her husband goodbye as he sailed to Hawaii, where he served his country, sent her a steady flow of pictures, and penned a stream of letters to keep her company until he returned. They were married until he died, almost fifty years later. A memorable life.

Fifteen minutes before the funeral, I met the daughters in person for the first time. The gathered mourners had some stories to tell. The daughters described the day their mom accidently set the neighborhood grass on fire. Her adult grandson detailed the months when he had moved in to help her, but refused to serve as her chauffer, forcing her to drive again. A family friend vividly related the time she and her husband employed shotguns to scare potential intruders from their cabin. On and on the stories went. Attendees wiped away tears, doubled over in laughter, and wondered periodically how much to say with an unknown preacher in the room.

For my part, I spoke several well-loved psalms from memory, trusting in the sturdy and poignant words that had moved generations of people. Among them were these words from Psalm 103: "As for mortals, their days are like grass; they flourish like a flower of the field. . . . But the steadfast love of the LORD is from everlasting to everlasting on those who fear him." In church funerals these words are a healing balm over wounds rent by grief. But in that rented suburban ballroom turned funeral parlor, they seemed as out of place as a hip-hop tune at a country music jamboree. I felt like a hired DJ whose music selection was slightly off. The people attending responded with the sort of pleasant tolerance you see at a fifth-grade violin recital. They seemed anxious to move on to the post-service buffet tastefully arranged nearby. On a tight time schedule, I left for the Unitarian Church to lead the second funeral, feeling like a doctor who'd prescribed the wrong medicine at an hour of need.

I had already booked the first funeral for the woman from Texas when a woman called to ask if I would preside at a funeral for her daughter-in-law. Years earlier her son had been a regular drummer at our church. He loved hanging out with musicians, talking musical genres, and playing percussion. Because he was willing to play drums in any venue, he found himself playing at our church. First, he told me, he attended just to play music. But gradually he discovered that he believed the stories he was hearing. Over lunch one day he informed me, "I'm in." When he later moved to an apartment in a city twenty-five miles away, we gradually lost touch. Until his mother called to say he had died unexpectedly. Would I officiate at his funeral? For several months afterward, she attended our church, her face full of curiosity. And pain.

Four years passed before I heard her voice whispering on the phone again: "Would you do our family another big favor at a difficult time?" What mom can bear to bury her son and daughter-in-law before her seventieth birthday?

As a pastor I've done many funerals, but never before two in one day. Mourners were gathering when I arrived. Again, I was struck by the photographs carefully placed on tables lining the church hall. In one the woman posed smiling with her infant grandson. In a second, she sat wedged between her daughter and son, faces full of laughter. Next she was a teenager, pictured between her two younger sisters. My heart stopped when I saw her high school graduation photo. This was no dustbowl survivor. She was from my generation. We could have gone to high school together.

Again, I was taken by the stories told about her during the funeral. Her younger sister described how she functioned as a mother figure in their home, even grounding her for staying out past curfew. Her son described her as a loving, nurturing mom, spearheading pizza gatherings for the extended family, remembering birthdays and anniversaries, hosting Wednesday night family reunions, and directing the annual Friday-after-Thanksgiving shopping extravaganza. She was the adhesive that held the family together. She never missed a gymnastics practice or Little League game. Her family said she was such a master planner that they half expected her to find a way to plan her own memorial service.

Between stories, we sat silently listening to classic anthems of the 1970s. Art Garfunkel sang "Bridge Over Troubled Water." The Beatles sang "Let It Be." Then it was my turn. I expressed my sympathy to her family and friends, affirmed the stories celebrating her life, popped open a can of Diet Coke—the drink that never left her side—and then began with those same words from Psalm 103: "As for mortals, their days are like grass; they flourish like a flower of the field. . . . But the steadfast love of the Lord is from everlasting to everlasting on those who fear him." How would the psalmist's ancient words resonate with these mourners?

A friend of mine serves as volunteer chaplain for his small town's fire department. While we were away at a retreat with others, together dreaming of planting new churches where people can hear timeless stories of faith, he stepped out to receive a phone call. When he returned his face was white. A teenager had shot himself. Alerted by their friend's last text message, the teen's two best friends found him at home. He had taken his own life, just as he said he would. Now these teens were at the scene of the suicide and the parents needed to be found and informed.

Hardened, veteran fire fighters asked this chaplain to send help.

What do you say to grieving teens and parents about to return to a home that will never be the same? Emergency professionals endure a thousand hours of training. They attend seminars each year to ready themselves for their work. But in the face of such grief they were out of their league. A hundred miles away from home, the chaplain phoned pastor friends, begging them to help. They pleaded excuses—they didn't know the family. They weren't trained as chaplains. It wasn't their job. All the while his fire-fighting friends left urgent phone messages pleading for help, asking him to send a person with words to say. "Send someone," they pleaded. "Send *anyone*."

Hebrew scholar James Mays writes that in settings such as funerals, when words seem grossly inept, psalms provide genuine help. Psalms understand, and were often birthed in, such emergencies. They enable us to speak at life's worst moments, giving us God's own words to address such horrors. They train us in a vocabulary rigorous enough for the emergency rooms of our life and give us language to express our human frailty. Their words are "adequate to and honest about feelings of suffering, anxiety, alienation."[1]

Michael Perry is a volunteer fire fighter and author living in New Auburn, Wisconsin. In his book *Population: 485*, he writes about meeting his neighbors, one siren at a time. "How astounding, the number of people fate allows to float through this life never once confronting their own mortality. One of the benefits of the fire and rescue business, if you will have it, is a near-constant sense of vulnerability."[2] He describes the day he saw a man he once knew as a tattooed, tavern-clearing mound of muscle weeping in bed, hairless from radiation. He tells what it's like to kneel beside a wrecked car and see a burly forty-year-old shaking with pain and fear, and to realize that the last time he saw him was on a high school football field ramming his body like a weapon at the rival team. We float through life without confronting our transience, says Perry, and suddenly, there it is. He calls this state of denial *ignortality*. He and a handful of his neighbors answer call after call, doing what they can to help in every crisis. He remembers walking into one home "and seeing this little man looking up at me with such trust, and I thought one day I will be the little old man on the bed. And I hope my neighbors come when I call."[3]

In 1974 Ernest Becker wrote a book called *The Denial of Death*. The fear of death, he said, haunts the human animal like nothing else. We arrange our lives avoiding and repressing the most irrefutable fact in the world—that we're going to die. Our "workaholism," our obsessions, our passionate desire for success and approval flow from this fearful avoidance. His book was published to great acclaim, even winning the Pulitzer Prize. But 1974 was also the year Becker got cancer and turned to God. And it was the year he died. Even this writer who exposed the fear and denial of death couldn't avoid it. But we continue to try.

Most of us live in a state of *ignortality*, expertly ignoring our obvious mortality. Truth be told, most of us have an amazing capacity to deny reality. No, that attractive young woman who's too busy washing her hair Saturday night to accept your dinner invitation will not accept if you ask her again this weekend. No, that son of yours, despite hours of fatherly coaching, will never play professional baseball. No, your middle-age pot belly will not be hidden by that sensational Hawaiian shirt.

Four months before the Saturday of the double funeral I went skiing with six friends, an event we had planned months in advance. Arriving to six-foot snowdrifts at a friend's cabin in the Sierra Nevada Mountains, we were stunned by the alpine beauty. All evening our ski gang enjoyed our favorite adult beverages; homemade cookies warm from the oven; and plenty of salty, crunchy snacks. After a quick breakfast the next morning, we posed on the cabin steps for a "before" photo. Donning colorful ski jackets and holding our skis, we were unable to hold back enthusiastic grins. In a word, we were flourishing. Six of us then drove left to the nearby downhill ski resort. One drove right to cross-country ski at the resort with the "most miles of groomed trails in North America."

Cross-country skiing is not the epitome of daredevil activities. But neither is skiing solo high on the list of recommended activities, as I soon discovered. Stuffing two extra chocolate chip cookies and a power bar into my pack, I purchased my day pass and eagerly headed for the trails. An electronic sign at the trailhead flashed the conditions for the day: Epic. Even in my highly enthusiastic state I guessed their description was oversell. Maybe a bit icy, but *epic*? Instead of heading to familiar mountain trails, I took the trail less traveled. I pushed my two-week-old skis uphill on a connector trail that would lead me around a frozen mountain lake and then a beautiful mountain pass.

Climbing the incline felt good. My heart rate increased. My calf muscles throbbed. The skis slipped in the icy conditions, but I was managing to crow's-feet up the hill, feeling the inner smugness of a pseudo-expert. Three minutes later I was gliding down, faster than I had gone in years. My new skis were working. Gaining speed around a curve I had a fleeting thought—maybe I was going *too* fast. But another inner voice spoke louder: "Live the adventure. After all, the other guys are *downhill* skiing. What's the point of getting new skis if you're going to dawdle?"

Rounding the corner toward a steep downgrade, the edge of my right ski stuck for a second. A nanosecond. And I was airborne, launched forward into flight. I had fallen many times. But this time I landed head first. I found myself thinking, "So this is why some people wear helmets when they ski!" My shoulder tacoed on the hard-packed snow. I slid to a stop. That inner voice, so full of bravado and confidence just moments ago, now whispered, "You're an idiot." It kept on talking, "You're lucky to be alive. You just earned a trip to the emergency room." Still in denial I tested my body: my legs are OK. My torso is OK. My head must be OK; after all, I'm talking to myself." Then I reached for my ski. My collarbone cried for mercy. Pulling my weight up with my left arm, I saw that my new ski pole was now shaped like a question mark. I skied for four minutes that epic day.

Two hours later I sat in a waiting room. The doctor entered with my X-ray. I braced myself like a convict about to get his sentence. Here's your reward for four minutes of skiing like an eighteen-year-old when you're deep into your forties. Placing the film into a lighted box, he studied the shadows. His opening line was fine: "Just as we thought. You have a broken clavicle. These breaks normally heal on their own, with time." "Thank you, Jesus," I whispered. But his next sentence forced me off my one-way street of denial and down the dark alley of reality. "But for people your age, healing is not certain. I'd recommend surgery. People *my* age? *Surgery?*

I'm a fainter. I come from a long line of fainters. I'm convinced it's a sign of royalty, but I don't yet have medical proof to convince physicians. The blood drained from my face. I had to lie down on the examining room bed. Surgery? For skiing four minutes? Four weeks earlier I had preached a four-week sermon series on Psalm 103. One sermon focused especially on how this psalm helps us address our finiteness. "As for mortals, their days are like grass. . . ." I found it much easier to help our congregation face their *ignortality* than to face my own.

In the great scheme of life, a broken clavicle is a relatively simple setback. My dad first endured prostate cancer, then open-heart surgery. My younger brother has had surgery on his gall bladder, a leg crushed in a machine designed for corrugated cardboard, and a hip replacement. A three-year-old child in our congregation was diagnosed with a rare heart disease that will need monitoring for the rest of his life. A pastor friend served a nine-month stint as Army Chaplain in the U.S. Army medical command post at Landstuhl, Germany, where many brave young women and men begin their new life as amputees. What's a broken clavicle in the face of real misery?

Our church is across the street from an "active retirement community" with nine thousand homes, all built in the last eight years. Home buyers are relatively young, many in their fifties. They're lured with advertisements offering the perfect retirement. One home owner who attends our church calls it "geezer heaven." He says they have geezer golf, geezer art classes, geezer swimming lessons, and geezer vacation trips. Everything a geezer could want. I suppose in his scheme I provide "geezer spirituality." But he also said, "When we hear the sound of the ambulance coming into our village, we wonder if it's coming for one of our friends."

One Saturday during my sermon series on Psalm 103, a couple from the geezer community stopped by the church, asking for me. They had started attending our church five years earlier, on the Sunday we began to worship in our new facility. They were faithful church-goers, baking cookies for youth events, arriving early every Sunday. Over the years we shared meals and laughter. But one Sunday a team of dramatic readers prolonged its Sunday pre-service rehearsal, asking everyone to wait outside the sanctuary until they were finished ten minutes before the service began. That was a deal-breaker for this couple. They stopped attending our church. Now, a year later, they were waiting to meet with me in my office. "We have come to say goodbye," they told me. I was puzzled—we'd already been through this. Months earlier they had told me they wouldn't be attending our services. My face must have registered confusion. "I have brain cancer," announced the man. Their worry and fear showed in their faces. "We just came back from one last trip with our children. And now we're saying goodbye."

We cried together. We were sad. They told me about their family trip to Hawaii. Eventually we joked a bit and smiled. And then I told them about Psalm 103. I told them about the unmistakable way it reminds us that we are finite, but in words just as clear, it also promises that we can trust the God who is everlasting. After forty years together they were about to be separated, against their will. Could they trust themselves to the God whose love never ends?

Henry Francis Lyte was born in 1793 on a farm near Kelso, Scotland. His father deserted the family soon after making arrangements for Henry and his brother to attend school. Henry's mother then moved to London, where she and his youngest brother soon died. At school Henry's headmaster soon recognized his scholastic abilities, paying the fees to keep him enrolled and welcoming Henry to his own family for holidays and special meals. In effect, Henry became his adopted son. Henry grew up and became an Anglican priest.

Stirred deeply by the devastating illness and death of a fellow pastor and friend, Henry was transformed from a predictable, proper pastor into a poet with an edgy but comforting message. Lyte said of his friend: "He died happy under the belief that though he had deeply erred, there was One whose death and sufferings would atone for his delinquencies," adding, "I was greatly affected by the whole matter . . . and I began to study my Bible and preach in another manner than I had previously done."[4] Later, his own frail health forced him to move to Brixham, a fishing port of fishermen famous for their gallantry and daring in the stormy waters of the Atlantic. Among such sturdy people, he wrote an unforgettable hymn based on Psalm 103, a hymn that captures the faith of all who find themselves in unsafe places.

Praise, my soul, the King of heaven;
to his feet your tribute bring.
Ransomed, healed, restored, forgiven,
evermore his praises sing.
Praise him for his grace and favor
to his people in distress.

Praise him, still the same as ever,
slow to chide, and swift to bless.
Fatherlike he tends and spares us;
well our feeble frame he knows.
In his hands he gently bears us,
rescues us from all our foes.

And in one grand sweeping finale, he calls all creation
to praise this infinite, tender, saving God:
Angels, help us to adore him;
you behold him face to face.
Sun and moon, bow down before him,
dwellers all in time and space.
Alleluia, alleluia! Praise with us the God of grace!

After conducting the two funerals that summer
Saturday, I wrote to the grieving families. Repeating my
condolences, I wished them God's comfort and told them
how honored I was to participate in such a deeply personal moment. Both families responded with lovely notes
of appreciation. The daughters of the Texas-born mother
wrote, "We can't possibly express the comfort that your
words gave us yesterday. Our mother was a memorable
person, as evidenced by her friends and family spending
time honoring her memory. Many of our friends and family asked me where your church is, so you may see some
of them there. They all loved having you there to lead us
through the grief to the light that is God. We know Mom
is with him and our family, which gives us comfort but
does not yet ease our sadness. But yesterday's important
ceremony allowed the door to close softly behind us so that
we can get on with our new lives without she who loved
us most. . . ."

So perhaps this psalm didn't bounce off Teflon hearts after all. Maybe its words worked their ancient healing on all of us suffering with *ignortality*. Maybe that Saturday the gospel once again sounded with the clarity of a well-tuned Stradivarius.

PRAYING THE BLUES

PSALM 130

"That's the trouble with the world: we all despise ourselves."

—Charlie Chaplin

"I am not a painter."

—Michelangelo

Out of the depths I cry to you, LORD;
Lord, hear my voice.
Let your ears be attentive to my cry for mercy.
If you, LORD, kept a record of sins, Lord, who could stand?
But with you there is forgiveness,
so that we can, with reverence, serve you.
I wait for the LORD, my whole being waits,
and in his word I put my hope.

I wait for the Lord
more than watchmen wait for the morning,
more than watchmen wait for the morning.
Israel, put your hope in the LORD,
for with the LORD *is unfailing love and with him is full*
*   redemption.*
He himself will redeem Israel from all their sins.

—Psalm 130

Twenty-three times the local newspaper featured his mug shot on the front page. Six accusers pushed for his conviction. Media-following neighbors made assumptions, averting their eyes as he and his wife walked past. His unwelcome notoriety caused strangers to approach him at restaurants and ask, "Why don't you move away to another town?" He thought about it. A thousand times he thought about it. But he and his wife decided to stay.

We met two years before this barrage of undesired publicity. He and other city building committee members approved a slight change in the design of our church facility. We lobbied that night for the approval of more modest parking lot light fixtures, a savings of $40,000. That night he was a well-placed official, wielding authority to endorse or oppose building projects all through our burgeoning city. Now he had resigned his post under the dark cloud of sexual misconduct.

After the allegation against him became public, he was driving past our church one day when something (some One?) deep inside spoke to him: Drive into that church parking lot. He did. Later he phoned and asked me to come to his home and pray with him. In his family room a tangle of life's details tumbled out. He had been raised Mormon, divorced, and remarried. Successful in business, he was estranged from his children. Staring into my eyes he said, "The whole town is against me. People see me and walk away. Are you sure it's OK for me to come to your church?" He and his wife did come. Awash in fear and braced for rejection, they sat in the back row, scanning for reactions. During our afternoon conversation at his home, he repeated his request. Would I pray with him and his wife?

Bravely they stayed in town, attempting to keep their life, now under the microscope of the media, as normal as possible. Walking city sidewalks was a step of courage. Going to dinner was an act of valor. Each day brought its own deluge of rejection. Occasionally the deluge of shame was too much, and they would be submerged under a powerful tidal wave of emotion. One afternoon, when their sinking spirits dropped especially low, they visited the church unannounced, only to find the front doors locked. Desperate for a good word, they circled the building to my office in the back. Cupping their hands they peered through my office windows, intent on finding encouragement. I will never forget the intensity on their faces. Frantic for a kind face, searching for reassurance, they were searching for a scrap of respect. How do the drowning pray?

As the trial date approached, the publicity intensified. So did their church attendance. Days before his court date he asked, "Can you visit me during my trial? Will you pray for me in the courtroom?" As I entered the court, expecting a stately setting dominated by a raised, highly polished wooden bench against a backdrop of ornate murals, I found instead the sort of low ceiling and cheap steel seats you find in a typical department of motor vehicles waiting room. Seated between friends, his wife broke ranks to greet me. He pulled away from his lawyer. "I knew you'd come," he said. "Can we pray now? Here, while the trial's on break?" How do the drowning pray?

Months after the trial ended, happily for them, another couple in church included me on an email they sent to a group of friends. It began, "Sorry if this is a shock . . . but it has been quite a sudden shock for us as well." Details from the day's doctor appointment and those of the last three weeks poured out. The young father began with what he called the good news: "The prognosis is good. We have the best oncology surgeon on the west coast. He has done this procedure at least one hundred times." The cancer is the *good* news? He went on to report that specialists had found two types of cancer on his wife's appendix. The first was believed to be contained. The second, a low-grade type of cancer, had burst, spreading cancerous cells "throughout her abdomen."

Then followed the bad news. In four weeks she would undergo an all-day surgery. Doctors would remove part of her large intestine and lymph nodes in the appendix area for the first tumor. From the second tumor, he said, "there is benign mucinous material (MM) growing slowly in her abdomen. It will continue to grow if not removed and possibly constrict organs in the future. It could someday change from benign to malignant."

His message relayed more bad news than a young family could endure. But it wasn't finished. He went on to describe in detail the treatments that would follow his wife's surgery, including grueling rounds of chemotherapy. Her hospital stay would be nine to eleven days. Her recovery time at home would last another six to eight weeks. He added, reverting to his native tongue, "It's not clear on the follow-up game plan at the moment . . . one step at a time."

My mind rewound the family's story. Eight years ago this couple had given birth to twins, a joyful event that had them seeking out fellow "parents of multiples," all in search of the specialized encouragement they needed to meet the challenges of double (or triple) infant parenting. Three years earlier, the husband's mother had died of a rare liver disorder, a disease that was then detected in other family members. The previous summer, in response to the discovery of this same liver disease, the husband donated one of his kidneys to his sister. His scars were barely healed, and now it was his wife's turn. How much could one family take? I wondered. In a P.S., he added, "FYI, none of the following information has been told to the children (especially the cancer word). All they know is that mom is getting her tummy worked on after her appendix burst." How do you pray when a tidal wave sweeps you off your feet, when your pristine world suddenly becomes a heap of chaos?

In their distinctive distress, each of my friends experienced a custom version of a universally known feeling. They joined a chorus that rises from every continent and every century in every language. In Spanish Psalm 130 begins, *A ti, Señor, elevo mi clamor desde las profundidades del abismo*. Martin Luther translated it in German as *Aus der Tiefe rufe ich, Herr, zu dir. Herr, höre auf meine Stimme, laß deine Ohren merken auf die Stimme meines Flehens!* "Out of the depths I cry . . ." *The Message* says simply, "Help, God, the bottom has fallen out of my life." Generations of musicians know this psalm by its Latin opening, *De profundis*.

Who knows what type of flood whelmed the psalmist? What caused him to set down such prized words in a world without paper or ink? A thousand generations later, his poetic image articulates the cry of breaking hearts. We're drowning—in a sea of red ink, in a loveless life, in a barrage of physical ailments. We're sinking—in public scorn, in self-loathing, in the quicksand of guilt. We're fraught and frantic, distressed and desperate. We're plummeting, and we cannot stop ourselves.

Few psalms, writes James Mays, have such a remarkable history in the life of the church. Tracing its history offers an unexpected sense of belonging in the misery that often isolates us. We are alone in our grief, our shame, our melancholy. As the old spiritual says, "Nobody knows the trouble I've seen." Out of this isolation, Psalm 130 invites us to join a chorus of fellow sufferers who unwillingly but reflexively sing its refrain. The moments of our most beleaguered loneliness give way to a sense that we belong to a historic assembly that raises its voices "out of the depths."

One of our fellow choristers in that refrain seems an especially unlikely candidate to utter a prayer for the drowning. Raised in an aristocratic home, Augustine was wealthy, literate, urbane, and unusually smart. Raised as a Christian by his devoted mother, he was entranced by the allures of pagan society. He played truant, skipping school to see Roman cockfights, delighting in the darting attacks and skilled parries, the victor's crowing, the limp wings of the loser. He thrilled to see the hound chasing its prey. As a young man of sixteen, he conceived a son with his mistress. With pretty words he coaxed her to leave the church she loved and move in with him. But even after thirteen years together, he refused to marry her or to have another child, considering her social standing beneath him. For nine years he was an eager member of a group of heretics.

What drew him back to faith was the rhetorical skill of a bishop. He became a skilled theologian, an eloquent preacher, and a highly regarded bishop. In his forties, he wrote *Confessions*, the book many consider to be the first autobiography. It's an amazing window into a fourth-century human soul.

But after all his years of sermons, churchmanship, and service, Augustine felt hopelessly contaminated. He passed his final days in a plain, barely-furnished room. As vandals besieged the gates of his beloved Hippo, he prayed in unadorned solitude, deluged by the memories of sins he had committed during his ministry. Regrets flooded his mind. Feeling polluted, he pored over his failed attempts at love and peace. Grace, not sin, was Augustine's main word. Yet in his final days he was desperate for a glimpse of such comfort. At his request, large-lettered copies of four psalms were fixed to the walls of his cell. Four psalms; nothing else. Seeing the words from his bed, he prayed them again and again, lamenting his sins as a bishop. A proven wordsmith and eloquent spokesman, he could think of no better way to express his heart's cry than to join this chorus: "Out of the depths I cry . . ."[1]

Like Augustine, John Donne was born into a life of privilege and carefree living. Often he acted the playboy, bedding women and writing brilliant ditties inspired by his favorites. He penned such gems as "A Defense of Woman's Inconstancy" and "Why do women delight in feathers?" (Answer: Women are "flighty.") An early portrait features him as a young man of means and social standing. His intricate lace collar, the gold-feathered motif on the sleeve of his mantle, and his folded arms display an air both confident and haughty.[2] A series of tragedies and missteps changed his fortune. His family's Catholic origins fell out of vogue with the changing British monarchy. Events beyond his control thwarted his enduring desire to secure a position in the royal court. He fell madly in love with Ann, a noblewoman far above his social standing as a modest court secretary, but secretly wed her anyway, violating both her father's wishes and the favor of the royals. His miscalculation in the highly stratified society of sixteenth-century England led him to prison and then a decade of poverty. Later, reflecting on his unwanted station in life, he griped, "My fortune hath made me such as I am, rather a sicknesse and disease of the world then any part of it."[3]

Desperate for a livelihood, Donne was urged by a friend to consider the priesthood. He demurred, believing that "certain irregularities" from his past disqualified him, and sought other ways to support his beloved Ann, the one constant in his life. Believing that their marriage had "transplanted (her) into a wretched fortune," a biographer notes, made Donne feel constantly guilty. She gave birth to a child almost every year of their marriage until her last pregnancy, ending with a stillborn, took her life as well.[4] Donne, many miles away, believed he witnessed her death in a vision, causing him to pen these words:

Batter my heart, three-personed God; for You
As yet but knock, breathe, shine, and seek to
    mend;
That I may rise, and stand, o'erthrow me, and bend
Your force, to break, blow, burn, and make me new.

I, like an usurped town to another due,
Labour to admit You, but oh! to no end;
Reason, Your viceroy in me, me should defend,
But is captived and proves weak or untrue.
Yet dearly I love You, and would be lov-ed fain,
But am betrothed unto Your enemy;
Divorce me, untie, or break that knot again,

Take me to You, imprison me, for I
Except You enthrall me, never shall be free;
Nor ever chaste, except You ravish me.

Donne's life had begun so full of promise—but now, for all his poetic skill, he could only pen his lament. Unable to secure steady employment, grieving first deceased children and now his wife, he was forced to face a bitter reality. And so, still believing himself unfit for ministry, he exchanged his poetic hopes for what was to be his true lot, taking holy orders in the Church of England. A devoted pastor, Donne served earnestly as a man "whose penitence was as real as his sins had been."[5]

Although Donne preached sermons on many biblical texts, the psalms were his favorite. Was his heart stirred by the camaraderie of his fellow poets, the psalmists? Was he following Augustine, "that blessed and sober Father," whose stormy youth made them kindred spirits, and whom he deeply admired? Reading the psalms in their original Hebrew, the Latin Vulgate, and various English translations, Donne immersed himself in their inspired poetry. He often found comfort in Augustine's favorite, *De profundis*, repeatedly chanting its final two words, *copiosa redemptio*, full redemption, "as though they were a charm against all melancholic fears."[6]

As a poet, grieving father and husband, and Dean of London's St. Paul's Cathedral, Donne served his parishioners and his city as a horrible plague swept through the great city. During those dark days Donne plumbed the depths of human misery and spoke to people who were experiencing "the depths." His most famous lines explore the profound connection we feel for each other in our deepest losses.

> No man is an island entire of itself; every man
> is a piece of the continent, a part of the main;
> if a clod be washed away by the sea, Europe
> is the less, as well as if a promontory were, as
> well as a manor of thy friends or of thine
> own were; any man's death diminishes me,
> because I am involved in mankind.
> And therefore never send to know for whom
> the bell tolls; it tolls for thee.

Like Augustine and John Donne, Nick Wolterstorff is a philosopher and prolific writer. Speaking thoughtfully and creatively on subjects ranging from metaphysics to episte- mology and from the philosophy of religion to aesthetics, he has taught at Yale, Harvard, and Notre Dame and has published books on topics as varied as education, philoso- phy, art, ethics, and practices of belief. With colleagues he launched the Society of Christian Philosophers and the journal *Faith and Philosophy*. He's also a father who joined Donne and Augustine and thousands of less famous people in the chorus of *De profundis*.

Life was going well in the 1980s when Wolterstorff received a phone call from Europe on a particularly bright, sunny Saturday afternoon.

"Mr. Wolterstorff?"

"Yes?"

"Is this Eric's father?"

"Yes."

"Mr. Wolterstorff, I must give you some bad news."

"Yes."

"Eric has been climbing in the mountains and has had an accident."

"Yes."

"Eric has had a serious accident."

"Yes."

"Mr. Wolterstorff, I must tell you, Eric is dead. Mr. Wolterstorff, are you there? You must come at once!"[7]

For three seconds he remembers feeling "the peace of resignation." And then the pain: "cold burning pain."

Only twenty-five, Eric was full of life, gifted in math and science, and an accomplished artist. He was in Germany writing a Ph.D. thesis on the origins of modern architecture. And he was climbing mountains. He loved the mountains. He loved them more than his studies, more than visiting famous cathedrals, even more than his art. That love, says Wolterstorff, was his death.[8]

After Eric's death, Wolterstorff began to write. He wrote to record his pain. He wrote to process his feelings, and he wrote to honor Eric. "It's so wrong, so profoundly wrong, for a child to die before its parents. . . . How can I bury my son, my future, one of the next in line?" Flying across the Atlantic Ocean, on the grim paternal assignments of claiming Eric's crumpled body and signing documents of release, he wrote, "The plane was full of youths going to Europe for the first time—loud, boisterous, exuberant. I burrowed into my seat." Standing before the library in which Eric researched his Ph.D. dissertation, he wrote, "I see nothing, no form at all, not even a trace . . . where he should be, I stare straight through."

When a bitter friend suggested, "Why don't you scrap this God business?" he wrote in his journal, articulating a reply for himself, if no one else: "Faith is a footbridge that you don't know will hold you up over the chasm until you're forced to walk out onto it. I'm standing there now, over the chasm. I inspect the bridge. Am I deluded that in God the question shouted out by the wounds of the world has its answer. . . . I cannot dispel the sense of conducting my inspection in the presence of the Creating/Resurrecting One."[9] Weeks after Eric's death, reflecting on the tangle experienced by every griever, he wrote, "Suddenly here he is again. The chain of suggestion can begin almost anywhere . . . everything is charged with the potential of a reminder."[10]

And then one day, Nick and his wife, Claire, commissioned composer Cary Ratcliff to create a requiem in memory of Eric. Together the grieving parents had composed a text. Gathered mostly from biblical passages, they shaped their elegy into six parts. Their custom funeral hymn begins with the awfulness of death and ends with Christian hope. Part II begins,

> Like a bird alone in the desert
> or an owl in a ruined house
> I lie awake and groan,
> like a sparrow lost on a roof
> Ashes are the bread that I eat,
> I mingle tears with my drink. (Psalm 102)
>
> From the depths I cry to you, O Lord,
> give heed to my lament. (Psalm 130)[11]

In their requiem the Wolterstorff family join the chorus of parents and children, poets and preachers, agnostics and believers—a chorus from every continent and every age. Their variation on this ancient lament links them musically to a band of overwhelmed sufferers.

There's something about Psalm 130 that pulls in composers and hymn writers. It's as if our sinking soul needs a melody to heal. Too raw for speech, our emotions crave harmonies. The list of composers drawn to *De profundis* forms a bewilderingly diverse musical hall of fame: Mozart and Mendelssohn; the Swiss composer Arthur Honegger; Alan Hovhaness, the American composer of Armenian and Scottish ancestry; the French Baroque composer Michel-Richard Delalande; the Czech Neo-Romantic Vitezslave Novak; Johann Sebastian Bach; and the head-banging metal sounds of the Polish death metal band Vader.

Few theologians appreciate the potent duet of text and music like the great Reformer Martin Luther. "Next to the word of God," Luther wrote, "the noble art of music is the greatest treasure in the world." He composed music designed to stir the faith of the German masses, putting the great themes of faith to melody, including a three-stanza confession of faith based on the Apostles' Creed and a hymnic version of the Lord's Prayer. In 1523 he wrote a hymnic version of Psalm 130:

> From depths of woe I raise to Thee
> the voice of lamentation;
> Lord, turn a gracious ear to me
> and hear my supplication;
> if Thou iniquities dost mark,
> our secret sins and misdeeds dark,
> O who shall stand before thee?

When finished, Luther sent it as a sample to his colleagues, encouraging them to write psalm-based hymns for use in worship. He called Psalm 130 one of the "Pauline Psalms"—along with Psalms 32, 51, and 143—because it highlighted his favorite Pauline theme: forgiveness by grace apart from human works. A year after first putting it to music, he added a fifth stanza, further developing its theme of salvation by grace alone:

> Though great our sins and sore our woes,
> His grace much more aboundeth;
> His helping love no limit knows,
> Our utmost need it soundeth.
> Our Shepherd good and true is He,
> Who will at last His Israel free
> from all their sin and sorrow.

Luther's expanded version became a featured component of many Lutheran liturgies. It was widely used at funerals, including that of Frederick the Wise, his loyal friend and protector. And when Luther's own corpse was en route to its final resting place in Wittenberg, his close friend and fellow pastor, Justin Jonas, handed copies to those who came to pay vigil, and the thousands who flocked around his casket sang it together.[12]

Inheriting this German Lutheran tradition, Johan Sebastian Bach was a prodigy, the youngest child of a German musical family. His father directed the *Stadtpfeifer* or town musicians, teaching his son to play violin and harpsichord. His uncles, all professional musicians, were church organists, court chamber musicians, and composers. Orphaned at ten years old, he moved in with his oldest brother, Johann Christoph Bach, a church organist. Johann

Sebastian wrote countless arrangements of Lutheran hymns, many based on the Psalms, including "In Thee Have I Hoped, Lord," based on Psalm 31:2-6, and "By the Rivers of Babylon," based on Psalm 137. Bach's Cantata no. 38, *Aus tiefer Not schrei ich zu Dir*, first performed in 1724, was his version of Luther's Psalm 130.

Two hundred years after Bach, a young Estonian helplessly watched as his country was absorbed by the Soviet Union. Growing up in scarcity seemed to feed his inner hunger for music, all kinds of music. Beginning at age fifteen, Arvo Pärt began composing, using countless musical styles and eventually scoring music for over fifty films. Pärt's "De Profundis," says music critique William Edgar, takes listeners into the realm where "deep calls forth unto deep" and "time is a faculty of life in the Spirit." Scored for a choir of male voices, organ, and chimes, it moves slowly from the haunting plea "Out of the depths have I cried unto thee, O Lord," to the stirring assurance "Let Israel hope in the Lord: for with the Lord there is mercy." Finally it turns to the settled promise "He shall redeem Israel from all his iniquities." Pärt's interpretation of this ancient psalm shows the power of sparse language, says Edgar, and so it becomes an ideal affirmation of countercultural values, reflecting Pärt's adult rediscovery of the Christian faith of his upbringing. In joining himself to the words, stories, and liturgy of the Russian Orthodox Church, Pärt discovered a way to be both honest about the evil surrounding him and to finally rest in God's sovereign love.[13]

Walter Brueggemann, professor and veteran psalm-lover, writes that Psalm 130's powerful appeal over many centuries and in many traditions comes from its glaring honesty. It voices dis-ease, and to its voice we may add our

own particular dis-ease. Speaking from a place of significant weakness, this prayer boldly challenges the Ruler of
Heaven. One assumes that an underling ought to address
a Sovereign in "suitable dress" and with proper, well-
rehearsed etiquette. Can an inferior, utterly weak, helpless
and miserable, presume on the Monarch to listen, let alone
act? Brueggemann calls this a "psalm of disorientation."
Rather than deny his gloomy reality, the ancient pray-er
expresses its entirety, a tangle of dread and alarm. And yet
as he prays, he rereads his ominous state through the reality of God's sovereignty, steadily moving toward a more
expectant conclusion.[14] It is this journey, starting in the
depths but turning toward hope, that is so appealing to a
publicly accused city father and a young mother with cancer in her abdomen, to singers in a Polish heavy metal band
and a poet who has lost his beloved wife.

Eugene Peterson frames the astonishing appeal of
Psalm 130 this way: It offers "not so much as a trace of
those things that are so common among us, which rob us
of our humanity when we suffer. . . . No glib smart answers.
No lectures . . . no hasty Band-Aid treatments covering up
our troubles so that the rest of society does not have to
look at it. Neither prophets nor priests nor psalmists offer
quick cures for the suffering: we don't find any of them telling us to take a vacation, use this drug, get a hobby. Nor
do they ever engage in . . . the plastic-smile propaganda
campaigns that hide trouble behind a billboard of positive thinking. . . . [Instead] the suffering is held up and
proclaimed—and prayed."[15]

As Cabinet Minister in the English Parliament and
Chief Secretary to the Treasury in the 1990s, Jonathan

Aitken discovered the power of Psalm 130 in the most unlikely place. Aitken's smiling face was well-known throughout Britain. But with sudden, surprising speed, his fame became infamy. Within a year of his cabinet appointment, he resigned his office. Hours later he was in a prison van heading to Her Majesty's Prison Belmarsh, perhaps London's toughest jail.

Like that of all prisoners, Aitken's entry to the jail included a grueling set of rituals: strip search, mug shot, psychological interview, confiscation of possessions, and the issue of ill-fitting prison clothes—all carried out amid the earsplitting shouts and jeers of his fellow prisoners. His arrival was documented by televised news reports. Within minutes of his appearance he became the favorite target of the prison's most vicious, expletive-laced catcallers. Aitken's heart froze. He felt "utterly helpless and totally vulnerable." Each succeeding hour was a nightmare.

In that frightening place, anyone might impulsively turn to a higher power. Aitken knelt on the cell's concrete floor and tried to pray, but he felt his prayer drowned by the menacing shouts around him. Then he remembered that in the moments before his transport to prison, a friend had placed in his pocket a calendar style booklet called "Praying the Psalms." Completely desperate and hopelessly alone, he turned to the page for the date of his arrival. The psalm for the day began "Out of the depths . . ." Instantly, Aitken says, "a warm comforting assurance flooded over me." He no longer felt hopeless, fearful, exposed. The author of this psalm, he sensed, had "been there before me." By God's help, he found a way to climb out of his depths. At a moment of acute fear on the worst day of his life, Aitken said, he "stumbled on the riches of the psalms in a prison cell."[16]

Eighteen months into his sentence, and only two weeks before his release, his prison friends asked him to give a "valedictory talk." The event was well-advertised and attendance swelled beyond the customary Christian prisoners. Just before Aitken was to speak, a great shock swept over the gathered inmates. Into the prison chapel walked "The Big Face." Every British prison has "The Big Face," a name assigned by prisoners to the jail's most feared and vicious prisoner. "The Big Face" at Belmarsh prison was a gang boss near the end of his sentence for a chain of revenge killings. At his unexpected entrance many attendees grew noticeably nervous, the speaker included. Uneasy but determined, Aitken rose to speak. Building his talk around Psalm 130, he described the profound way its words had shaped him during his prison time. It had great meaning, he said, for anyone suffering in the depths. It was his favorite psalm and the favorite of Augustine, Luther, and Calvin. The Big Face, Aitken said, nodded gravely. Near the end of the talk, The Big Face became visibly moved; Aitken noticed tears trickling down his cheeks. When Aitken followed his talk by offering a prayer, The Big Face joined in with a booming "Amen." Afterward, he drew Aitken aside, asking whether he could come over to his cell the next night and say his piece over again to a couple of his mates.[17]

Aitken must have looked considerably tense at the prospect of an evening with "The Big Face" and his two close associates, so the gang boss magnanimously expanded his guest list: "And, John-o, to make yourself feel comfortable, why don't you bring a couple of your mates along with you? I mean, how about bringing those geezers you said liked the psalm so much? Augustus, and What's-it, too, if they're friends of yours in the B-Wing."[18]

Even without the presence of Augustine or Luther, Aitken said, Psalm 130 went down well the second time round in The Big Face's cell. Although that surprised him that night, his surprise faded with time as he came to understand the universal appeal of the psalm. The more a person knows the psalms, the more they trust their "power to speak to a wide variety of people and situations."[19]

My friend at church, the mother of three young children and the bearer of two rare kinds of abdominal cancer, went into surgery as scheduled. Keeping vigil with her anxious husband in that downtown hospital were faithful supporters who had come from nearby and far away. Friends had driven down from suburbs, and another flew out from Iowa. Her dodgy brother-in-law drove in from the agricultural valley. Amid doctors' reports they kept anxious watch throughout the extensive surgery. When I arrived we participated in the ancient ritual of hospital talk: updates from the doctors, comparisons to related surgery procedures, and bantering with fellow vigil keepers to pass the time. We found an empty space outside the waiting room where we held hands and prayed, taking our place with British prisoners and Bach concert-goers as we joined the ancient chorus: "Out of the depths. . . ." We prayed through the middle repetition, "my whole being waits," and we kept praying all the way to Donne's favorite final words reassuring us of the Lord's "full redemption."

Our friend survived the surgery. Her recovery was a bit longer than doctors had originally predicted. There were days she thought she'd never leave the hospital, moments she felt too exhausted to rise from her bed. She had hoped to be released in a week; it took more than two. The doctors, it turned out, had only partially prepared her for her surgical aftermath. They had strategically left unsaid a few of the worst parts of the recovery process. They'd discovered that patients, when they were given a full picture of the surgery's aftermath, often chose to skip the surgery, even if that surgery was necessary to save their life.

Six months after returning to health, this young mom, now free from abdominal cancer, and her husband reflected on their journey through the depths as part of our morning worship service. They described their ordeal in enough detail that several front-row parishioners started to wobble noticeably. They remembered the strong, practical love of friends who brought meals to their home, ran errands, and shuttled their children to practices and school.

After expressing her copious gratitude to friends, the young mom added a personal reflection. "During recovery," she said, "while floating in and out of anesthesia, my friends said my language was often profound." Catching sight of a smirk crossing her husband's face, she said, "What?" Gently he corrected her in front of their church family: "I think you mean to say that in and out of anesthesia your language was *profane*." The entire church burst into laughter. And why not? What had begun as a cry "out of the depths" was now a story of "full redemption."

That positive and playful ending would be the ideal way to end a chapter that began with trauma. But in real life, there's always more to the story. Four months after causing church-wide hilarity, the husband sent another email. "K was admitted to the hospital Monday night with bad abdominal pains. Doctors confirmed that she has obstructions from lesions and twists in the intestine from her major surgery one year ago tomorrow. . . . She is doing good: stable, and alert . . . just throwing up every few hours or so." After a week she returned home to her waiting family, but soon returned to the hospital for a surgery to remove scar tissue.

A few weeks later I asked the young mom how things were going for her and her family. "Instead of 'Living the dream,'" she said, "our new motto is 'Living the life of Job.'" They had just returned from the Appendiceal Cancer International Conference. She called it a wonderful time to compare notes, asking "insider" questions like "What organs are you missing?" and "How many surgeries did you have?"

Years earlier and quite unexpectedly they had joined the community of "parents of multiples." This time they had become, equally unexpectedly, members of a community of people with a rare form of cancer. Along the way, without always being conscious of it, they had joined a chorus of those who begin in the depths but end by speaking of "full redemption." *De profundis.*

THE CENSORED PSALM

PSALM 137

*"With God anything can be said, without God nothing is heard.
Without God what is said is not said."*

—Elie Wiesel

*By the rivers of Babylon we sat and wept
when we remembered Zion.
There on the poplars we hung our harps,
for there our captors asked us for songs,
our tormentors demanded songs of joy;
they said, "Sing us one of the songs of Zion!"
How can we sing the songs of the LORD while in a foreign land?
If I forget you, Jerusalem, may my right hand forget its skill.
May my tongue cling to the roof of my mouth if I do not
    remember you,
if I do not consider Jerusalem my highest joy.*

Remember, LORD, what the Edomites did on the day
　　Jerusalem fell.
"Tear it down," they cried, "tear it down to its foundations!"
Daughter Babylon, doomed to destruction,
happy is the one who repays you according to what you
　　have done to us.
Happy is the one who seizes your infants and dashes them
　　against the rocks.

—Psalm 137

In two weeks his master's thesis was due, and Carnegie-Mellon University is no place to be late with a thesis. Deep into his studies of Greek and Roman mythology, he took a break to attend an Easter Vigil service at Pittsburgh's St. Paul Cathedral. Fellow churchgoers offered looks of hostility, not hospitality. His overalls, long hair, and T-shirt made him look so suspicious that a nearby police officer frisked him for drugs after the service. It was 1970. Trust between the establishment and college students was razor thin.

A lifelong member of the Episcopal Church, he had considered becoming a priest. Instead, he was a university student who staged liturgical drama for the Cathedral of Saint John the Divine in New York. Whether it was a sermon series or a two-day conference on the environment, said his rector, he turned it into theater.

Later, reflecting on his Easter vigil experience, he wrote, "I left with the feeling that, rather than rolling the rock away from the tomb, they were piling more on. I went home, took out my manuscript, and worked it to completion in a nonstop frenzy."[1] Compelled by the impending deadline and fueled by his fascination at the joy he found in the gospels, he threw himself into the work. At twenty-two years old, he was writing the work of his life.

John-Michael Tebelak's thesis project was presented off-off Broadway in a theatre called Café la Mama. It featured pop songs and lyrics set to music by cast members whose hippie garb and clown themes inspired unwanted controversy. Tebelak later explained that he derived his clown analogy from *Feast of Fools*, a book by Harvard Divinity School professor Harvey Cox. A year after its debut, Tebelak teamed with Stephen Schwartz to give the show a commercial run off-Broadway. In two months they rewrote the script into a musical they called *Godspell*.

Decades later the musical's most enduring song is "Day by Day," a resetting of an Episcopal hymn written in the thirteenth century. But its oldest lyrics are included in the utterly moving song "On the Willows." Sung against the backdrop of the Garden of Gethsemane, as the Jesus character is saying a heartfelt goodbye to each cast member, its vocals are tender and haunting: "On the willows there we hung up our lyres, for our captors there required of us songs and our tormenters mirth. . . . How can we sing . . . the Lord's songs in a foreign land?"[2]

Stretching across three thousand years, these timeless lyrics first appeared in Psalm 137. They evoke a tragic sense of melancholy, a desperate longing for the better days of home. But for all their poignancy, these lyrics borrow only part of the original psalm, the *safe* part. In a surprising irony, this famous musical, set in the great art-loving, avant-garde city of New York, quotes lines far tamer than the original biblical text. Why might a young New York City artist, writing what has been a controversial musical in the minds of conservative religious people, feel it necessary to "fix" the text so that it is less provocative than the original?

Perhaps no biblical text is more chilling than Psalm 137. Its nostalgic beginning soothes like a lullaby, but it ends on a white-hot note with a finishing sentence we might expect from heavy metal screamers. It's the stuff of nausea and nightmares: "Happy is the one who seizes your infants and dashes them against the rocks." If psalms are supposed to *lift* our thoughts and inspire us, if psalms should be prayers safe for use by the whole family, if psalms should offer motivational maxims that can inspire frame-worthy works of needlepoint, then this one fails miserably. Psalm 137 explodes any preconceived notion of prayer etiquette.

Psalm 137 has been dodged and discreetly edited for generations. Even such a stellar Bible interpreter as Augustine softens its violent ending by turning it into an allegory. Instead of picturing the psalm's infants as actual babies, he suggests that we imagine them as a kind of metaphor for our own temptations. For example, if we find ourselves prone to anger or increasingly lazy, better to grab these sinful inner tendencies while they are still like little babies in our souls and dash them to pieces.

Oxford professor C. S. Lewis, for decades an atheist before his reluctant conversion to Christianity, applied his relentless and clear-minded logic to volumes of books and articles. But he too proposed a possible double meaning that avoids the terrible picture of dashing actual babies against the rocks. Our petty indulgences and small resentments are "like babies" that seem so tiny and helpless but may one day grow into selfishness and hatred. Against all such "pretty infants," says Lewis, we ought to follow the advice of the psalm: "Knock the little bastards' brains out."[3]

Nothing in the psalm's melancholy opening lines prepares us for its spiteful end. During a year-long study of the psalms, our California congregation encountered all sorts of psalm imagery. One challenge was to present the favorite metaphors and images of the Psalter in a way that is accessible to biblical novices, people with no Christian memory. What does it mean for such people to consider Zion the "joy of the whole earth" or to "consider well her ramparts, view her citadels" (48:2, 13)? How do we, emerging from a suburban mall, pray "May he remember all your sacrifices and accept your burnt offerings" (20:3) or "May the praise of God be in their mouths and a double-edged sword in their hands" (149:6)? Together we explored how these ancient prayers from Palestine could become our own.

But nothing could ready us for Psalm 137. The day we read it as our text, the congregation gasped audibly at the last line. Eugene Peterson calls it "a can of black spray paint defacing a memorial in white marble."[4] We want to ask, "Who let such hostility in our prayer book?" Maybe no one.

For centuries, many in the Christian church routinely and regularly recited every verse of the entire Psalter. Churches birthed in the Reformation drew up metrical versions of all 150 psalms so that the congregation might together sing them in their entirety. Some traditions pledge to sing the psalms—the entire psalms and only the psalms—in their worship services. Others, including the Eastern Orthodox Church, established the Divine Office, a helpful framework to encourage the ancient practice of reading all the psalms in a weekly or monthly routine.

So did the Roman Catholic Church, providing the Liturgy of the Hours, a practice that provided generations of believers with a way to recite the entire Psalter during a four-week period. Until 1970, that is. Then it was revised with a new format omitting three psalms entirely—Psalms 58, 83, and 109—and skipping verses from nineteen other psalms. As the *Apostolic Constitution* issued by Pope Paul VI in 1970 explains, "in this new arrangement of the psalms some few of the psalms and verses which are somewhat harsh in tone have been omitted, especially because of the difficulties that were foreseen from their use in vernacular celebration."

Commenting on this post-Vatican II deletion, William Holladay wryly notes, "In other words, parts of the psalms that did not seem offensive to reciters who only half understood them in Latin are now to be omitted when the reciters hear what they really mean in their own language."[5] More than 15 percent of the Psalter didn't make it to print. Instead these ancient, divinely inspired words were deleted by editors who either deemed them more upsetting than inspiring or determined that modern readers would find them too offensive to pray.

Psalm 139 was one of those affected by such editorial cutting. Its introspective beginning, "You have searched me, LORD, and you know me," was judged helpful and appropriate. But eighteen verses later the psalmist's sentiment was deemed out of bounds,

If only you, God, would slay the wicked!
Away from me, you who are bloodthirsty!
They speak of you with evil intent;
your adversaries misuse your name.
Do I not hate those who hate you, LORD,
and abhor those who are in rebellion against you?
I have nothing but hatred for them;
I count them my enemies.
If only you would slay the wicked!

But what if verses 19-22 are, in fact the pinnacle of the psalm? What if they voice the writer's most passionate loyalty to God? Then our first-reaction squeamishness would backfire, keeping us from understanding the psalm's intent or experiencing its meaning. Might the editing imply a hidden, unspoken belief that such phrases are remnants of the psalmist's uneducated and backward spiritual past, one that we state-of-the-art people have outgrown? Centuries removed from the psalm's original setting, do we consider ourselves too hip, too insightful, too sensitive to pray its untamed words? Could it be that our well-intended cutting signals an inner snobbishness, a sense of spiritual superiority and belief that we have advanced beyond some of the phrases Jesus and the disciples took to be divinely inspired? Might it we be wiser to work to understand them instead?[6]

Rastafarians are not so timid. First appearing in 1930s Jamaica, Rastas have wedded the Bible to a liberation-themed social and political philosophy. Nathaniel Murrell, author of numerous articles on Caribbean religion, says Rastafarians took the narratives, psalms, and prophetic sections of the Old Testament and Africanized them, using them to express a powerful new sense of identity and to nurture hope in the liberating work of "JAH," the living God. For Rastas, Murrell writes, the psalms have special appeal, their poetic beauty inspiring rhythms and truth-filled dialogue. Instead of censoring laments like Psalm 137, Rastafarians adopt them as favorites, using their lyrics to announce their desire to break free from generations of humiliation and domination. Fighting words voice their pain, still throbbing after years of colonial rule, and express their determination to bring social change. Occasionally Rastafarians use the psalms to offer praise: "It is a good thing to give thanks unto JAH, and to sing praises unto thy name" (Ps. 92:1), but primarily they use psalms as tools to chant down the enemy, whom they call Babylon. The psalms provide revolutionary vocabulary against injustice and corrupt political systems.[7]

In 1969, a singing group called *The Melodians* sang Psalm 137, giving it a Rastafarian voice under the title "Rivers of Babylon." The song remained a local Caribbean favorite until a 1975 disco version, sung under the influence of reggae star Bob Marley, became an instant global hit. Later Marley himself recorded a reggae version of the psalm.[8]

Instead of dodging laments as embarrassing remnants of a less civilized past, Marley and his fellow Rastafarians tied their own story to the story of the original Hebrew singers who, like their ancestors, were ripped from their home and forced into slavery. In the radical words of Psalm 137, Murrell writes, they hear a revolutionary call for justice and hope for what often seems to them a hopeless cause, the liberation of an oppressed people. So Rastafarians sing these typically censored psalms in their entirety. They sing to end generations of silent surrender, pushing themselves toward freedom. They sing to end what they see as the divine silence on the rape of Africa during centuries of slavery, colonialism, and the oppression of Africa's children. Like the original Hebrews exiled in Babylon, they cry for justice, resonating with the passion of the psalm's shocking ending.[9]

Few other psalms can be as clearly connected to their original setting. Forcibly removed from their homeland by Babylon's imperial policies of relocation, these exiled Jews composed this melody in order to cling to hope. Walter Brueggemann suggests that this psalm functions as a way for the community to keep hope alive, to act out and transmit to the next generation the hate-laced yearning that belongs to each dislocated person. Their venom didn't bring the Israelites sudden help. It didn't empower them to storm the gates of their oppressors. But they drew power, Brueggemann says, from a vision of a homecoming to peace and freedom that seemed remote, but never in doubt. Singing this lament, then, connects us to an ancient and ever-continuing community. We become practitioners of hope, hoping against enormous odds, hoping against injustice, stubbornly hoping even when the temple is an ashen crater. The psalm's fixation on Jerusalem is a way to take a counter-cultural stand, to act in a way that says life is not controlled by Babylon. Brueggemann admits that this psalm is not the noblest moment in the Bible, but it serves a purpose, reminding us that God is King. This psalm voices a veteran faith that knows what it costs to beat off despair for a lifetime. It is the way to entrust our most precious hatreds to God, who will take them seriously.[10]

The magisterial documentary *Shoah* begins with the story of Simon Srebnik. The film's opening frames show the forty-seven year-old Srebnik in a small boat on the Narew River. As he passes along the water, we hear him softly singing a folk song from his past. But this is no idyllic scene. Soon we learn that Srebnik is one of two survivors of the Chelmno death camp; the trip along the Narew returns him to the site of his internment. The return reenacts his ordeal. During his imprisonment, SS troops forced him several times each week to row a flat-bottomed boat along the river and sing to entertain them and the Polish villagers nearby. Srebnik's present song "echoes what he sang thirty years ago." Walking the empty space where the death camp once stood, he says,

It's hard to recognize, but it was *here*. They burned people *here*. A lot of people were burned *here*. Yes, this is the place. No one ever left *here* again. . . . No one can describe it. No one can recreate what happened *here*. Impossible? And no one can understand it. Even I, *here*, now . . . I can't believe I'm *here*. No, I just can't believe it."[11]

Some elderly villagers remember how the Germans made him sing on the river, a toy to amuse them. He had to do it. So he sang, but his heart wept. Srebnik's ordeal raises the ancient question: how can we sing songs in a foreign land?

The stinging poetry of Psalm 137 carries an eyewitness account of an atrocity. A powerful nation bullies a smaller one; when a much-loved and besieged capital falls, soldiers loot and kill, and they carry survivors into exile. All the while, Israel's ancient antagonists, the Edomites, cheer on the looters. Soldiers tear babies from their mothers' arms, grab them by their little feet, and dash their brains against the rocks. In his commentary on the psalms, Derek Kidner says, "There is ample evidence that 'to dash in pieces their little ones' was a common enough sequel to a heathen victory." He goes on to cite a similar event that happened at Bromberg during World War II. Soldiers took Jewish children by their feet and struck their heads against the wall.[12] How could an eyewitness ever forget such cruelty? Memories like these cannot be ignored or pacified by simplistic answers.

Melissa Harris-Perry remembers sitting in a pew at Trinity United Church of Christ in Chicago, Illinois, on September 16, 2001. Gathered with fellow parishioners that first Sunday after the terrorist attacks in D.C. and New York, she remembers feeling a particular kind of terror. Six months pregnant with her first child, she realized that her daughter was coming into a world marked by a violence she found scary and unpredictable. Arriving at church that morning, she remembers how sad and unusually quiet Trinity was. And she remembers her pastor's words. Years later, in the heat of the 2008 campaign for the United States presidency, that homily became infamous as the "Chickens Coming Home to Roost" sermon and ignited a national debate on civil speech. But for her it would always be remembered as "the sermon on Psalm 137," a word delivered in a time of anger and fear relating to dispossessed people terrorized by their enemies.[13]

We can readily stomach Psalm 137 as a lament for things lost, as a song of the exile. It's that last verse that sickens and disturbs us. But we need Psalm 137, all of it, in our prayer repertoire. We need it as a way to express anger that can roil in us, a way to voice our hostility and hate. Most of us are powerfully tempted to cover our hate, perhaps most of all in our prayers. How can our smoldering hatreds be allowed to erupt next to our pious thanksgivings and heartfelt intercessions? The Psalter provides us with words to pray our hate. There is no human emotion that cannot and should not be brought before God.

Eugene Peterson writes that in a world of sometimes great, radical evil, hate is often the first sign that we care. It is the emotion that can make us jump to our feet, shouting for justice. In a world gone soft and unfeeling, where we grow callous to reports and images of pain, sometimes hate can be the only emotion tough enough to penetrate our protective padding. For that reason hate needs to be prayed instead of suppressed. "Hate is our emotional link with the spirituality of evil. It is the volcanic eruption of outrage when the holiness of being, ours or another's, has been violated. . . . [W]e commonly neither admit or pray our hate; we deny it and suppress it. But if it is not admitted it can quickly and easily metamorphose into the evil that provokes it."[14]

The psalms don't stir up or legitimize hate, they simply acknowledge it and use it to get us on our feet, ready to work against oppression. Drawn into solidarity with victims in our linked-in world, we pray for a nephew ambushed in Afghanistan, a cousin molested in Serbia, a young blogger imprisoned in Asia.

Developing the stomach for such authentic prayer requires us to abandon our hunger for a spirituality oriented toward sentiment—the only flavor of prayer many Christians find digestible. In contrast, Psalm 137 forces us to experience evil directly, to grow beyond our appetite for the kind of overly romantic prayer we mistakenly imagine is symbolized in the psalm's opening lines. Expanding our prayer menu can be difficult, causing heartburn even among well-trained theologians and pastors. As Petersen reminds us, "It is easy to be honest before God with our hallelujahs; it is somewhat more difficult to be honest in our hurts; it is nearly impossible to be honest before God in the dark emotions of our hate. . . . The way of prayer is not to cover our unlovely emotions so that they will appear respectable, but expose them so that they can be enlisted in the work of the kingdom."[15] It takes a great deal of faith to entrust our deepest needs to God. It takes even more to entrust to him our deepest hatreds.

While teaching a seminary class on prayer, Patrick Miller asked class members to prepare their own imprecatory prayer in the style of Psalm 137. When students gathered the next time to discuss what they had written, they reported that attempting to write such a prayer had been an extremely emotional experience. Many simply could not bring themselves to do it, and none found a way to write about their own anger or plea for vengeance. The students who did manage to complete the project offered prayers of rage and solidarity with others who had suffered, for example, women who had been raped or abused.[16]

These pastors-in-training have a great deal of company. Many veteran believers can't imagine offering such a prayer. Like speaking a foreign language, it feels like a clumsy and dizzying experience outside the spirit of our typical prayer life. Miller suggests that we turn the question around. Rather than asking whether we could ever justify praying such hate, assuming that such a prayer is a rational decision and a matter of choice, what if instead we were to ask whether such tangled, hateful thoughts can be uttered any *other* place. Isn't prayer the only place to let our hate loose? He points to the victims of the Oklahoma City bombing who shouted and wept for joy at the conviction of Timothy McVeigh. Family members rushed to offer testimony describing in detail their own children's horror as a way to convince the jury to sentence McVeigh to death.[17] Rather than encouraging violence, does white-hot prayer offer a way to both let hate go and hold it back?

Far too honest to settle for a sanitized version of faith, the psalms allow us to pray life as it is, not as we wish it to be. They teach us how to grapple with evil, to hate the malice we see or experience. They coach us to understand that a spiritually alive person *feels* anger on behalf of the oppressed. Thank God that the Psalter's original Hebrew editors dared to take us to a deeply honest place where evil is more twisted and tangled into the fabric of life than we might have ever feared, or guessed.

Several years ago I was visiting my alma mater and picked up a copy of the weekly student newspaper. The front page carried the autobiographical story of a student who had attended the birthday party of a friend and drunk too much alcohol. When a fellow student, whom she had dated a few years earlier, phoned to ask if they might spend time together that evening, she said, "What I really need is a ride home." She doesn't remember the ride home. She remembers being brought home, and then running to the bathroom to throw up. The next thing she remembers is him raping her. After blurting to a friend what happened, she was coaxed into reporting her ordeal. She endured a rape exam. Her counselor held her hand during the invasive procedure. She cried. She took medicine to try to prevent STDs. Later she filed a police report. Her bruises were photographed and officers took a statement. The detective told her she had a very strong case against her attacker.

The following week, she says, "I simply went through the motions, made public appearances, finished my school work, and cried." Then she got a phone call she hopes someday to forget. Her male "friend" had gone to the police with a defense attorney, telling them a story far different from hers. Because she'd had a blackout, her testimony was deemed insufficient. The bruises from her assault were not enough to prove his guilt. Devastated at the news, she could not move for hours. How did God let this happen? Why was justice not served? Thousands of students attend that college, but it wasn't large enough for her to avoid seeing her assailant. Panic attacks plagued her when she glimpsed so much as the back of his head. She remembers feeling utter terror at discovering they were in a building together, or seeing his car in a campus parking lot. Nightmares plagued her for months. One night she woke up five times, each time seeing his face over her. Other mornings she awoke screaming. She has endured dark, disturbing emotions previously unknown to her. She has had suicidal thoughts. Some nights she can only lie flat on the floor, exhausted. She has pushed away dear friends, lashed out at people trying to help, and hurled things in rage, wishing evil on the man who did this to her.

Reading her courageous reflections, I found myself wondering what I would do if she were my daughter. Or sister. Or friend. How would I pray? Sometimes hate rises, unplanned. Sometimes it is the proper response to what we see. Praying only polished prayers squeezes our prayers into a narrow place where our faith can only gasp for air and then suffocate. The student's courageous story helps us see the ancient wisdom of this psalm, to see the complete wrongheadedness of any well-intended "psalmectomy"[18] that would make us miss what God intends as a gift.

On some level, I suppose, we're all fakers. We all dress up to play believer before God, denying the anger that simmers just under the surface of our piety. This stunningly concrete psalm teaches us a new way to pray. "Happy is the society whose cocaine dealers drop dead." It helps us to imagine the neighborhood child, once a gifted violist and academic star, who has become an addict, sullen and prone to violence. Maybe not knowing any cocaine dealers, we feel no personal vengeance. But the psalm helps us to imagine, and to pray with those who do.

The young victim at my alma mater dodged permanent self-pity. Slowly her hate is turning into something else. She writes,

> Being a Christian means that I have a greater responsibility than simply making it through the day. I have to acknowledge that drinking in excess like I did that night was a mistake on my part. My drinking does not in any way excuse my rape or provide justification for what he did, but drinking made me weak, made me vulnerable. But God is asking something more of me than acknowledging my damaging behavior. He is calling me to forgive. He is repeatedly prodding me with the conviction that someday I must look this person in the eye and tell him that I forgive him. And he's making it so that I cannot deny His presence in the situation. God has worked within this person to cause [him] to finally claim responsibility. God has answered prayers in such a specific way that I can no longer deny his existence. And this week, God enabled me to finally release my hatred and give this person over to him.[19]

Her grace astounds me. Forgiveness is always a miracle. That any victim can pray for her rapist and wish him well is a wonder, a divine phenomenon. But for those who do not yet feel her magnanimity, on days her forgiveness thins to almost nothing, for anyone who was raped just last night, there is Psalm 137—a scandal only to those who have never suffered.

BATTLE HYMNS

PSALM 144

"But the book of Psalms possesses a certain winning exactitude for those who are prayerful."[1]

—Athanasius

". . . in the Psalter . . . you learn about yourself. You find depicted in it all the movements of your soul, all its changes, its ups and downs, its failures and recoveries."[2]

—Athanasius

He trains my hands for battle. . . .

—Psalm 18:34

*Praise be to the L*ORD *my Rock,*
who trains my hands for war, my fingers for battle.
He is my loving God and my fortress,
my stronghold and my deliverer,
my shield, in whom I take refuge,
who subdues peoples under me.

—Psalm 144:1-2

Hundreds of bodies lay freshly buried on a French hillside. Others still floated in the English Channel— each a raw reminder of the D-day beach invasion just two days earlier. German gunfire had poured from pillboxes high and safe atop seaside cliffs, tearing into thousands of valiant young recruits clawing up Normandy's cliffs. As one veteran remembers, "Landing crafts were hit. Bodies were flying everywhere. There was blood on the edge of the water; the beach was just running with pure blood."[3]

Back in the bureaucratic safety of a United States military building, rows of secretaries type telegrams to the loved ones of the fallen. Each begins with heartfelt sentences offering condolences and the assurance that their deceased died bravely and for a just cause. As a thousand typewriter keys click words of sorrow onto army stationery, one observant secretary notices that three telegrams will be sent to the same address. A mother in Payton, Iowa, will soon learn that her son Peter was killed on Utah Beach, her son Sean was shot down on Omaha Beach, and her son Daniel died in New Guinea the week before. Overwhelmed with compassion for this unknown mother, the secretary begins to tremble. Gathering the telegrams, she brings them to her commanding officer. Quickly the news works its way up the chain of command until it's finally presented to the U.S. Army's Chief of Staff, General George Marshall.

"There's a fourth brother who parachuted in with the 101st Airborne somewhere in Normandy," reports a staff officer. "We don't know where. Is he alive? We don't know." "Ah, damn it," growls Marshall. Sensing costly compassion in Marshall's gravelly reply, a tough-minded staffer urges military protocol, "No way can we know where in the hell he was dropped. Assuming Private Ryan even survived the

jump, he could be anywhere. In fact, he's probably KIA."
He finishes with a tactical flurry: "And frankly sir, we go
sending some sort of rescue mission heading throughout
swarms of German reinforcements and they're going to be
KIA too."

Marshall listens. He harrumphs. And then he motions
his staff members to gather round his desk. From its top
drawer he pulls a book. A Bible? From it he takes a single
page. "I have a letter here," he informs his subordinates,
"written a long time ago to a Mrs. Bixby in Boston. Bear
with me." And he begins to read. "Dear Madame, I've
been shown in the files of the War Department a statement of the Adjutant General of Massachusetts that you
are the mother of *five* (here Marshall pauses for emphasis)
sons that have died gloriously on the field of battle. I feel
how weak and fruitless must be any words of mine that
would attempt to beguile you from the grief of a loss so
overwhelming. But I cannot refrain from tendering to you
the consolation that may be found in the thanks of the
Republic they died to save."

Putting the letter down, Marshall goes on to quote
from memory, "I pray that our Heavenly Father may
assuage the anguish of your bereavement and leave you
only the cherished memory of the loved and lost, and the
solemn pride that must be yours to have laid so costly a
sacrifice upon the altar of freedom. Yours very sincerely
and respectfully, Abraham Lincoln."

Finished, Marshall grimaces. His advisors keep silent,
awaiting his word. Teeth clenched, eyes focused, he
announces, "That boy is alive. We are going to send some-
body to find him. And we are going to get him the hell out
of there."

So begins the movie *Saving Private Ryan*.[4]

Back on the hills of Normandy, now three days removed from D-Day, Captain John H. Miller receives Marshall's order. He selects seven crack Army rangers, each with special skill for the errand and they set off on foot with orders to bring home a grieving mother's last son. They slog through rainstorms, encounter German snipers, mingle with wounded and dispirited Allied troops, and find two privates named James Ryan. Neither is the one they are looking for, so they keep looking. Along the way they do what soldiers do. They poke fun at each other. They torment their commanding officer. And they complain about their assignment. What sort of person are they saving? Is he worth their seven lives?

In the French village of Neuville the soldiers come upon a frantic mother and father in their bomb-wrecked home. Standing in a house missing its roof and outer wall, the anguished parents beg the Americans to transport their young daughter to safety. A heated argument splits the group. Private Carparzo wants to oblige: "It's the decent thing to do." But Captain Miller refuses. The platoon has a mission; they can't accept responsibility for a child. During their heated exchange of verbal artillery, Carparzo gently accepts the girl from her father's outstretched arms. At that moment a German sniper shoots him in the chest. Carparzo falls, badly bleeding. Pinned by the sniper, his colleagues, barely a few feet away, are unable to do anything but watch his life ebb away.

Through one camera we watch Carparzo die; through another we see the German sniper selecting his next victim. Then we hear the memorized words of a second sniper, the company's own Private Jackson. During D-Day's valiant push up the cliffs of Omaha Beach, while shooting German soldiers barely visible from the cliff, Jackson had quoted verse 19 of Psalm 22: "Be not Thou far from me, O Lord: O my strength, haste Thee to help me." Now, as Carparzo bleeds his life away, Jackson peers through the scope of his rifle, barely rising above his barrier. Softly he prays the first verse of Psalm 25: "O my God I trust in Thee, let me not be ashamed, let not my enemies triumph over me." Then Jackson pulls his trigger. He doesn't miss. "We got him," exhales one of his military brothers. Another mutters, "This Ryan better be worth it."

The following day the rangers find *the* Private James Ryan of Payton, Iowa. He's part of a haggard group of paratroopers defending the French village of Ramelle. Their orders are to secure a bridge, one the German infantry desperately needs. Their ragtag group has limited weapons, no commanding officer, and barely a handful of exhausted men. Private Ryan refuses to abandon his company. The soldiers sent to find Ryan nod knowingly. Perhaps, just perhaps, this private is worth the sacrifices they've made to find him.

Captain Miller assumes command at this new post; together they prepare for imminent attack. Their plan is to lure German tanks into a trap they've set in the rubble-filled streets. Private Jackson is placed in the village bell tower, armed with a sniper's rifle and a 30-caliber machine gun. As the well-armed German troops advance, Jackson again works his deadly skill. He shoots, quoting Psalm 144: "Blessed be the Lord my strength which teacheth my hands to war, and my fingers to fight." He shoots again, and continues: "My goodness and my fortress, my high tower and my deliverer. . . ." He shoots again. ". . . and my shield and he in whom I trust." After the next shot, a rare miss, he shoots again and continues "... who subdueth my people under me. ...." Then he looks up to see a tank aimed at him and shouts a warning, "Parker, get out!"

————————————

Over the centuries countless soldiers, like Private Jackson, have leaned on the psalms' steadying presence during battle. In 1588 "The Grand and Most Fortunate Navy" left Spain's shores to reclaim England for its Catholic monarch. Twenty-two warships accompanied by 108 converted merchant ships set sail, believing their cause was just. Daily prayers for success had been offered for three years. Ships were named after the apostles, and their crews abstained from vice, immorality, and foul language. Each sunset the men sang the *Ave Maria*. The standard flying from the lead ship bore their motto, the words of Psalm 35:23: "*Consurge et evigila in iudicium meum Deus meus et Domine in causam meam.*" ("Awake, stand up to judge my quarrel, avenge Thou my cause my God and my Lord.")[5] A short time later, this impressive fleet was scattered and destroyed. Ravaged by ill timing and ill wind, their demise became a glorious event in English history, a victory for which British citizens had prayed the psalms as well, especially the words of Psalm 3: "Lord how many are my foes, how many increased that trouble me."

Soldiers shaped by the psalms frequently fight on opposite sides. Few battles in the American Civil War were as pivotal or lethal as Gettysburg. On the Confederate side was General Robert Edward Lee. A top graduate of West Point Military Academy, Lee distinguished himself as an exceptional soldier. Early in 1861 President Lincoln asked him to command the entire Union Army, a post

Lee declined when his beloved Virginia seceded from the Union. Lee led the Confederate army instead, quickly proving his tactical skill at the battles of Fredericksburg in 1862 and Chancellorsville in 1863. He frequently visited his troops, who often received him "with a silence that was almost reverent."

Once, when informed that his chaplains had offered "most fervent" prayers on his behalf, Lee's eyes filled with tears. Choked with emotion, he replied, "Please thank them for that, sir. I warmly appreciate it. And I can only say that I am nothing but a poor sinner, trusting in Christ alone for salvation, and need all the prayers they can offer for me."[6] Into every combat of his storied career, Lee carried his prayer book. Every page showed regular use, but the most worn page, marked by a small strip of paper serving as his bookmark, includes Psalm 144:1, the psalm reading for the thirtieth day: "Blessed be the Lord my strength: who teacheth my hands to war, and my fingers to fight." Lee carried his prayer book with him every day from 1846 until 1864, when he needed to exchange it for another because the type had grown too small for him to read.[7]

Opposite Lee and his Confederate comrades that day was Joshua Lawrence Chamberlain. A gifted student, he taught himself Greek in order to attend Bowdoin College. There he met Harriet Beecher Stowe and listened to her reading what would become *Uncle Tom's Cabin*. Chamberlain became a staunch opponent of slavery. Both attended First Parish Church of Brunswick, Maine, listening to sermons and regular readings from the psalms. After graduation, Chamberlain studied at Bangor Theological Seminary (Maine) before returning to Bowdoin to serve as its professor of logic, rhetoric, and theology. When the Civil War began,

Chamberlain, whose forefathers had served in the American Revolution and the War of 1812, wanted desperately to enlist. Although college administrators tried to prevent him, he would not be refused. In 1862, Chamberlain requested and was granted a leave of absence to study languages in Europe. Instead of crossing the Atlantic, Chamberlain reported immediately to Maine's governor, who sent him to muster with the 20th Infantry.

After twelve hours of relentless marching his regiment arrived at Gettysburg and entered the thick of battle to hold Little Round Top, the extreme left of the Union line. Five times Chamberlain's troops beat back the brave, determined men of the 15th Alabama. He knew there would be a sixth. Desperately low on ammunition, as they re-grouped for yet another battle, Chamberlain ordered a bold bayonet charge down the hill so astonishing that his troops captured twice their number of prisoners. Which of the regularly repeated psalms from First Parish Church guided his valor? Did he repeat David's fearless words from Psalm 18: "For by Thee I have run through a troop; and by my God have I leaped over a wall"? Did he shout Cromwell's anthem: "Let God arise and his enemies be scattered" (Psalm 68:1)? Or did he whisper the opening words of Psalm 91 that he spoke later in a speech dedicating the Maine memorial in the fields of Gettysburg: "He that dwelleth in the secret place of the most High shall abide under the shadow of the Almighty"?

The list of those who lean on psalms during times of war includes the Huguenot armies who repelled charges and delivered assaults with a psalm on their lips. It includes the sentries who were posted and relieved to the chant of Psalm 3—"Lord, how are they increased that trouble me"—during the French Revolution. It includes Benjamin Franklin, who, when the American Continental Congress received word in 1776 that the British had bombarded Boston, read Psalm 35: "Contend, Lord, with those who contend with me; fight against those who fight against me." And it includes Winston Churchill, who quoted from Psalm 112 to address the joint houses of the United States Congress in the threatening days of December 1941: "He shall not be afraid of evil tidings: his heart is fixed, trusting in the Lord."[8]

Perhaps it is not surprising that people would turn to a psalm to steady themselves in the chaos of combat. What may be more surprising are some of the ways the psalms have been linked with war.

In 1115, at the ripe old age of twenty-five, the son of a mid-ranking aristocrat established a new monastery at Clairvaux and became its first abbot. Bernard was a visionary, a man of tremendous conviction and energy. For the next forty years his enterprising style and deep piety shaped not only his Cistercian Order but the entire church. A counselor of popes, an advisor to kings, and a key monastic reformer, Bernard influenced the politics and faith of Western Europe as few others had. Single-handedly he prevented a split papacy. His sermons stirred fellow monks to fervent faith, urging them to convert *themselves* to the true faith.

But in a strange blend of monastic piety and military zeal, Bernard also used his expansive powers of political pressure and religious sway to launch the second Crusade. In a letter intended for mass distribution, he wrote:

Since therefore your land is fruitful in brave men, and is known to be full of robust youth . . . gird up your loins manfully, and take up arms in zeal for the Christian name. Let not your former warlike skill cease, but only that spirit of hatred in which you are accustomed to strike down and kill one another and in turn be overcome yourselves. . . . Take the sign of the cross and you shall gain pardon for every sin that you confess with a contrite heart. . . .[9]

He went on to quote Psalm 59:11: ". . . scatter them by thy power and bring them down, O Lord, our shield. . . ."

At the time of the Crusades, a pilgrimage to the Holy Land was considered an act of high devotion. Pilgrims traveled from Europe to Palestine along danger-filled routes in desperate need of policing. After the first Crusade, eight knights offered themselves to the patriarch of Jerusalem to offer such protection. Bernard promoted their cause, and with his influential lobbying, the fledgling order of the Knights Templar received papal recognition in 1128.

In the spiritual directory he wrote for the Knights Templar, Bernard outlined many rules that paralleled those followed by his Cistercian monks. Before they patrolled the pilgrim route with swords and mail, the knights took vows of chastity, poverty, and obedience. In places, though, his instructions to them veered sharply from standard monastic practice. By fighting in holy wars, he said, the knights would become instruments of divine justice to reestablish God's order. He urged those who found themselves in the thick of battle to set aside gentleness and pray the words of Psalm 139: "Do I not hate those who hate you, O Lord? Am I not disgusted with your enemies?"

Echoing Psalm 91, he instructed them to be unafraid of an opponent's greater numbers, for "on numerous occasions they had seen one man pursue a thousand, and two put ten thousand to flight." "I do not know if it would be more appropriate to refer to [the knights] as monks or soldiers, unless perhaps it would be better to recognize them as both," he said. "Indeed they lack neither monastic meekness nor military might . . . they are picked troops of God, whom he has recruited from the ends of the earth."[10]

We are deeply troubled by this tendency to point swords at an enemy's throat while quoting warlike verses from the psalms. But even more disturbing, ultimately, is the presence of those warmongering words in the first place. Is any connection between the psalms and combat distressing?

Matthew Rothschild thinks so. He's a widely published gadfly who edits *The Progressive Magazine*, a self-proclaimed "leftwing magazine of investigative reporting, political commentary, and cultural coverage" that promotes itself as a leading voice for peace and social justice in the United States. No one was offended when President George W. Bush quoted Psalm 23 in his nationwide speech after the attacks on September 11, 2001. But a few years later, the political weather had changed. Moments after hearing Bush's second inaugural address, Rothschild analyzed it in search of "hidden passages" Bush might be using to appeal to his evangelical religious base. Zeroing in on Bush's line "Freedom is the permanent hope of mankind, the hunger in dark places, the longing of the soul," Rothschild was apoplectic. It was, he fumed, a thinly disguised quote from Psalm 107: "He satisfies the longing soul and fills the hungry soul with goodness, such as sit in darkness. . . ." According to Rothschild, Bush was seeing himself as "God's efficient little delivery boy, God's UPS man." And he wasn't the only one who complained: former Reagan speechwriter Peggy Noonan called Bush's speech "heavenish" and claimed that it left her with "a bad feeling."[11]

Of course George W. Bush was not the first president to quote a psalm in a wartime inaugural address. At his second inauguration Abraham Lincoln spoke of the war on everyone's mind. All dread it, he said; all seek to avert it. Each side "reads the same Bible and prays to the same God; each invokes [God's] aid against the other." And then, having already twice quoted the gospel of Matthew, Lincoln pointed his countrymen to a psalm: "Fondly do we hope, fervently do we pray, that this mighty scourge of war may speedily pass away. Yet if God wills that it continue until all the wealth piled by the bondman's two hundred and fifty years of unrequited toil shall be sunk, and every drop of blood drawn with the lash shall be paid by another drawn with the sword, as was said three thousand years ago, so still it must be said, 'The judgments of the Lord are true and righteous altogether.'" That last sentence is from Psalm 19:9.

After Lincoln was shot down on Good Friday, April 14, 1865, points out historian Mark Noll, Americans found it irresistible to see Lincoln's political accomplishments in a religious light, to imagine him as the "savior" of the Union. It seemed a likely characterization. With only slight exaggeration, friends said that Lincoln knew by heart many of the psalms, much of the book of Isaiah, and the entire New Testament. He was a leader of remarkable virtue with extraordinary spiritual insight. By all accounts Lincoln read the Bible regularly during his entire life, quoting from it extensively in many addresses. "It is one of the great ironies of the history of Christianity in America," writes Noll, "that the most profoundly religious analysis of the nation's deepest trauma came not from a clergyman or a theologian but from a politician who was self-taught in the ways of both God and humanity."[12]

Thrust into a war he didn't want but couldn't avoid, Lincoln first viewed the Civil War only as a political struggle to preserve the Union. But over the course of the war, says Noll, Lincoln "came to regard it as a crusade for truth and right. He spoke of the United States as 'the last, best hope of the earth,' of its citizens as 'the almost chosen people,' and of the War as a test to see if a nation 'conceived in liberty . . . can long endure.'"[13]

But even in view of a figure as revered as Lincoln, the gadfly's question remains. Can any commander or soldier quote the psalms in wartime without turning themselves into "God's UPS man"? To put it another way, can the psalms be rightly applied to war? Or are they only *mis*applied? Was Bush, as Rothschild raged, acting out of misdirected pious pride when quoting a psalm in the context of war? Was Lincoln? Private Jackson? Or were they simply joining a long line of leaders and ordinary citizens who have turned to the familiar words of the psalms to steady themselves in times of personal and national crisis and turmoil—especially in times of war?

No one is exactly sure who first wrote Psalm 144. The title "Of David" may mean that Israel's most famous commander wrote it himself. Or it might be that one of David's admirers wrote it in the style of David. Either way, it's remarkably unoriginal. It includes at least five lines from

Psalm 18, two from Psalm 33, and phrases from Psalm 8, Psalm 24 and others.

Like many psalms, Psalm 144 accents God's role as king. The metaphor of God as Monarch of the World is the main metaphor in the Psalter. As King, God shepherds his people (Psalms 23, 28, 78-80, 95, 100). As King, God judges his people and all the nations of the world (Psalms 93-99, 137). Also as King, God is the commander-in-chief who leads his forces into battle. God is a general who rallies the troops, a military champion who fights on behalf of his oft-threatened, battle-weary troops. Psalm 18 portrays God as a divine combatant of remarkable prowess. Psalm 24 sounds like the pre-battle litany of an army preparing for war. And Psalm 68 evokes the treasured image of God as the great warrior who strikes down mighty Pharaoh and his army, and whose victory established his saving reign in the world. Steeped in the tradition of these psalms, the writer of Psalm 144 offers a new work, a collection, a montage of memories designed to inspire a new outbreak of trusting prayer. James Mays points out that Psalm 18:44-45 tells of "a David whom the Lord empowered against foreigners. The composer of Psalm 144 must have found in these verses a promise for his own time," arranging these well-known and treasured images to assure the faithful that God would respond to their new time of need.[14]

Above all, God is the King who *acts*. In the psalms divine action isn't abstract theory but practical help. Providing such help is the way any king vindicates his reign. As *the* King, God acts on behalf of specific people in specific places. So is it too much of a stretch to think of God assisting Private Jackson as he picks off German soldiers? Of God supporting a well-read classics professor as he leads the charge at Gettysburg? Or of God inspiring a new knight to live out Psalm 115?

Two of my friends found themselves in the middle of a war. Each experienced the psalms in his own way. Billy and I met ten years ago when we formed a posse of prayer with two other local pastors, all church planters. We met each week to seek advice, admit our foibles, tell tall tales, and rejuvenate our spirits. Besides being a devoted pastor, Billy is also a dedicated backpacker, a dependable soccer coach, and a chaplain in the Army reserve. We call him Billy. His unit knows him as Major Chaplain Steen. After almost twenty years in the military, Billy decided to resign his commission. Torn between devotion to his unit and dedication to his young church, Billy decided to leave his post and focus more energy on his congregation's building project. But the day he went to resign, the United States invaded Iraq—determined to find weapons of mass destruction and loosen the reigns of a maniacal dictator. Soon Billy and his unit were deployed to Landstuhl, Germany. There he ministered to traumatized young women and men who had recently lost limbs in battle, and to the hospital staff who cared for them.

His second deployment brought him a new kind of action. After processing at Fort Benning, Georgia, he flew to Kuwait City and boarded a C-130 military transport to Baghdad's international "Green Zone." Instead of feeling like a heavily protected haven, as he had envisioned, the Green Zone felt like the center of a bulls-eye. Its perimeter, a series of cement t-walls fifteen to twenty feet high, was the target of heavy and relentless mortar attacks. The previous spring two senior officers had been killed in the Green Zone; seventeen were injured. A trailer ten feet from the wall of Saddam Hussein's former "Believer's Palace" became "home." Billy reported directly to Lieutenant General Frank Helmick. The mission was to equip Iraq to be self-governing once again by training and rebuilding the Iraqi army and police and the political infrastructure. He and his fellow officers felt enormous pressure. Camp protocol allowed for a half day off each week, but everyone was working around the clock, determined to bring prompt and permanent change. The soldiers had been without a chaplain for three months and were especially eager for his arrival.

Arriving that first night on base after days of military style round-the-clock travel, Billy learned that the general had scheduled him to lead a service of remembrance for the seventh anniversary of 9/11 the following morning. A few months later, in a letter describing his new life to friends back in Sacramento, Billy wrote, "It is a remarkable place to be. There are over two thousand personnel in our command, and I am the only Chaplain. One of the great blessings I have found in serving our military personnel, both at Landstuhl and here, is that they are very, very appreciative of preaching. I have never enjoyed preaching more than this past year. Our chapels are literally packed." In another letter he reflected on what captured the troop's spiritual interest:

> There is no other text of Scripture that I have relied upon more than the Psalter for my ministry as a Chaplain, in both my work at Landstuhl and in Baghdad. I have prayed the psalms over the dead bodies of fallen soldiers, and at General Officer change of commands. We began every worship service in Baghdad for a year with the praying of a

psalm. Because so many were written in situations of such extremity, the psalms resonate powerfully with those in extremity. Often . . . what you truly need most is someone else who will pray for you. That's what the psalms do, they pray for us when we can't pray for ourselves. No wonder that Jesus, in his times of greatest extremity, prayed the Psalter, prayers prayed for him when he could not pray himself.

The wartime experience of my second friend was decidedly different. Like Psalm 144, Sam is remarkably hard to categorize. A youth pastor who owns almost thirty registered guns, he belongs to the National Rifle Association, coaches cross country, and loves Ford Mustangs and Harley Davidsons. He was born an Eritrean in Ethiopia. Threatened by Ethiopian soldiers patrolling city streets in search of Eritrean males, his father fled to find safety. Sam then moved with his pregnant mother and two preschool siblings to the home of an aunt, whose decent-sized house and ample backyard provided an ideal setting for an extended family. Sam's first memory is of an ordinary afternoon when the family was enjoying a meal in the rear of the home. Suddenly the front door was blown open by a loud explosion. An unknown object rolled across their living room floor. Understanding their peril, Sam's mother barked, "Get under the tables." As they complied a detonation rocked the house. When daylight returned, they saw that a grenade had transformed their living room into a wreck with no ceiling.

Escaping their war-torn country, Sam and his mother traveled for hours by foot, his mom carrying his three-year-old brother and two-year-old sister. Eventually they attached themselves to a sizable group of fellow refugees. One afternoon, while his mom and the other adults talked under the safety of tree branches, Sam and his sister wandered to a nearby stream to drink and play in the water. They were just beginning to enjoy themselves when it appeared that someone was skipping rocks in their direction. But it wasn't rocks. It was bullets. A pilot, spying movement below, had begun firing. Sam's mother raced from the bushes to cover their small bodies with her own. As bullets flew all around, she covered her children with a motherly blanket of protection and prayed.

Decades later, after living as refugees in the Sudan, after moving to San Jose to start a new life, after losing one brother to death and another to prison, Sam asked his mom what she had prayed during those trying days. Over and over he had heard her whisper, "O Christos, O Christos." Was there another prayer that sustained her as she carried three preschoolers through a war zone? Had Sam's mother grown up in a stable country with access to a printed Bible, she might have chosen a few verses from Psalm 144: "Part your heavens, LORD, and come down; touch the mountains, so that they smoke. Send forth lightning and scatter the enemy; shoot your arrows and rout them . . . deliver me and rescue me." But Sam's mother never heard this curious prayer of both soldier and victim. So, answering in her native Tigrinya language, she simply said, "Twenty-three." Surrounded by a war she didn't want, she prayed the only psalm she knew.

So it is; so it has always been. Refugees and chaplains, military heroes and political leaders—each seeing war through the lens of their own experience—each turn to the King for justice, for mercy, for *action*. Saving action.

Martin Tel is director of music at Princeton Theological Seminary. As a child he belonged to a congregation that encouraged worshipers to spontaneously select songs during its Sunday evening service. His father regularly asked to sing Psalm 68. The plodding Genevan tune did nothing to stir Martin's soul or satisfy his musical taste. To him it was boring and monotonous, a plodding country workhorse with tired, predictable steps. How, he wondered, could such a song have captured his father's imagination?

Years later, as an adult, Tel learned how the song had become so precious to his father and why his parents sang it with such exhilaration. They had grown up in the Netherlands during the dark days of World War II. Even with their homeland occupied by the German army, the Tels attended worship services at the Dutch Reformed Church. So did the Nazi soldiers. Standing in the back, the well-armed soldiers wanted parishioners to see the power of the German military even in church. But those uniformed soldiers standing in their swastikas had no clue that the Dutch worshipers, in the spirit of the psalms, were thumbing their noses at the Third Reich. Looking to their King for rescue, they sang the treasured Genevan versification of Psalm 68. With fervor. With gusto. With the delight that comes from a resilient faith, they sang "God shall arise and by his might/ put all his enemies to flight."[15]

Psalms don't pick sides. As prayers they offer themselves to all takers: Here. Take this prayer. It is for warriors. It is for victims. It is for a sharpshooter whose well-intentioned buddy lies bleeding. It is for a refugee mother who shields her children with her own torso. It is for a mother back home who is about to get dreadful news.

The psalm that begins with a cry of war ends with a blessing for peace and flourishing. The King is a shepherd and judge and warrior. But one day, on the King's watch, all war will cease.

So may your sons be "like well-nurtured plants." May your daughters be like "pillars carved to adorn a palace." May "our barns be filled with every kind of provision." May our sheep "increase by thousands, by tens of thousands in our fields." May our oxen "draw heavy loads." May there be "no more breaching of the walls, no going into captivity, no cry of distress in the streets."

May you belong to God.

LIVING APOCRYPHALLY

PSALM 151

"When we sing [the psalms] we are certain that God puts in our mouths these, as if he himself were singing in us to exalt his glory."[1]

—John Calvin

"In spite of the strong conviction, then, that the Psalms numbered 150, there was a contrary tendency to add 'just one more' or 'just a few more'! . . . Psalm 151 . . . is a bonus that only dramatizes the complicated story of how the separate psalms were collected, annotated, and translated by successive generations of Jews and Christians."[2]

—William Holladay

Mohammed fell into a cave.

The day before, his cousin Jum'a was tracking a stray goat when he spotted an opening in the rocky hills. Jum'a flung a rock into its mouth. But this time Jum'a's stone didn't produce the familiar sound of rock thumping off a cave floor. Instead he heard the crash of breaking pottery. It was dusk and the light too dim for good spelunking, so the boys agreed to return to the cave the next day.

In the morning light they saw an ancient storeroom. Five dust-covered jars lined one side of the cave, and three hugged the other. Most had covers still in place. The boys' hearts began to pound. Had they discovered hidden treasure? Pulses thumping, they studied each jar. Opening the first they found nothing. They opened the second. Nothing. Another was filled with red dirt, the type found everywhere in the surrounding caves and hillsides. At last they opened a jar containing ancient leather scrolls. Climbing from the cave with their discovery, the boys were unimpressed. What boy wants his buried treasure to be a tired-looking leather scroll?

Still, their find was promising enough to lug back to the family tent, where together the family unrolled the scrolls. While deciding what to do with their treasure, the Bedouins hung several from a tent pole, periodically showing the unfamiliar script to curious neighbors and friends. Eventually they took the scrolls to a dealer in Bethlehem who examined them for a few days and then told the explorers that their discovery was worthless. Unknown to them, the dealer had been warned that the scrolls might have been stolen from a nearby synagogue. Undaunted, the discoverers visited a nearby market, where a Syrian Christian offered to buy the scrolls. A sheikh who joined in the bargaining suggested they take the scrolls to Khalil Eskander Shahin, a cobbler and part-time antiques dealer. They sold several of the scrolls to him for seven British pounds (about $29 US dollars at the time).

During the negotiations, they left the scrolls in the hands of a third party who, thinking the text might be Syrian, contacted Syrian priests at nearby St. Mark's monastery. One of the priests quickly determined that they were not Syrian and asked the American School of Oriental Research for help in discerning the scrolls' origin. During those turbulent days, with gunfire randomly erupting throughout Jerusalem, most of the staff had evacuated. All except for one person. Graduate student John Trever was in Palestine to take photographs of Palestinian wildflowers. Recognizing the scroll as a form of ancient Hebrew, like the Nash Papyrus, the oldest biblical manuscript then known, Trever took a series of photographs and airmailed them to the world's best-known Ancient Near Eastern archeologist, William F. Albright of Johns Hopkins University. Albright cabled Trever back to tell him he was part of the greatest archeological find of modern times. The leather scripts from these and other caves became known to the world as the Dead Sea Scrolls, and are now known by the Arabic name for the region: Qumran. A few years later, in 1954, they were sold for $250,000 and brought back to Jerusalem for display at the Shrine of the Book at the Israel Museum.[3]

Who first hid the scrolls in that craggy cave? Years of excavations uncovered scrolls in ten nearby caves of the Qumran region, all in close proximity to a settlement unearthed by archeologists. None of that ancient community's own writing details their community life, but half a century's excavations offer clues. The community called themselves "sons of Zadok."[4] For two hundred years, beginning about 150 BCE, their exclusively male members devoted themselves to intense study of and obedience to Jewish law.

That first discovery by the two shepherd boys included commentary on Habakkuk, the community rule, and a scroll outlining events to take place at the world's end, called the War Rule. Many other biblical documents and commentaries were found in later digs. But far and away the most beloved biblical text found in the Qumran caves is the book of Psalms. More than thirty copies have been found in the eleven caves discovered to date, including at least some fragment of 115 of the psalms. These allow us to piece together a fascinating, if partial, understanding of this ancient community, especially their affection for the psalms. Most interesting of all, they offer clues to the editing process that ultimately formed the Psalter's present arrangement of 150 psalms.

Archeology is something like piecing together a giant jigsaw puzzle. Some scrolls, like the ones discovered that first day by Jum'a and Mohammed, are remarkably well preserved. Others were found crumbled into pieces over time, despite the cool cavern temperatures. William Holladay, Professor of Old Testament at Andover Newton Theological School in Boston, describes the most extensive Qumran scroll of psalms, which was discovered in 1956 and first unrolled in 1961. The scroll is leather. Its beginning is missing, but what is left measures thirteen feet long. The bottom of the scroll has eroded away, so the lower one-third of text is missing from each of its twenty-eight columns. Based on the handwriting style, experts estimate that the scroll was copied at the time of Jesus.

The text itself includes three surprises. First, it contains all or parts of thirty-nine psalms now included in our Bibles, but the sequence of these psalms differs significantly. Second, the text of individual psalms is not always the same as the traditional Hebrew text used to translate modern Bibles. And third, mixed in with psalms are other poetic texts, for example 2 Samuel 23:1-7, called "the last words of David," and psalms previously unknown to us: 151, 154, and 155.[5]

Psalm *151*?

This window into the early formation of the Psalter can be puzzling, even disturbing to those who prefer their religion fixed and orderly. Bible students call the sixty-six books of the Bible a *canon*, which means a fixed rule or order. But the Qumran treasures provide a unique vantage point for seeing the psalms in their ordinary, earthy originality. They invite us into an earlier world tied closely to human authors, hand-copying scribes, and editors. Strewn about on cave floors, stored carefully in lidded jars, and appearing in multiple forms, these fragments remind us of the profound humanness of the Bible, of how the psalms enter and serve our chaotic, disordered world.

The community at Qumran didn't have a corner on Psalm 151. One of the early and important manuscripts of the Greek Septuagint called the *Sinaiticus* has 151 psalms, closing with the subscription "The 151 Psalms of David," as if assuming that everyone knew there were 151 psalms. Another ancient text, *Alexandrinus*, includes Psalm 151 as an appendix with the superscription "This psalm is ascribed to David as his own composition after he had fought in single combat with Goliath."[6] Some early Latin and Coptic translations of the Bible also include Psalm 151, as do early medieval texts found in places we now call Ireland and Iraq. Several current ecumenical translations, such as the New Revised Standard Version, include it with the apocryphal books. Eventually the Eastern Orthodox Church accepted it as part of their canon, but Roman Catholic, Protestant, and most Jewish believers consider it apocryphal. Summarizing Psalm 151's history in and out of the biblical canon, William Holladay suggests that it "dramatizes the complicated story of how the separate psalms were collected, annotated, and translated by successive generations of Jews and Christians."[7] This apocryphal bonus adds to our understanding of the Psalter's divine inspiration.

Six hundred years after the Qumran community began, another desert-dweller appeared. He was a master of orthodoxy, a theologian of highest regard, a biblical scholar of sterling reputation. His enemies called him the Black Dwarf—and the diminutive, dark-skinned Bishop of Egypt was never short on enemies. Exiled five times by four different Roman emperors, he spent seventeen years of his forty-five year tenure as bishop banished from his parishioners. During periods of exile he wrote prolifically. His *Life of St. Antony* was a book so packed with spiritual dynamite that reading it helped pagans like Augustine convert to the Christian faith. More than anyone else, he shaped the early church's understanding of monasticism.

His treatise *On the Incarnation* set the underpinnings for the council and then the creed of Nicea, a conclave at which his fellows dubbed him "the noble champion of Christ." He made a deep impression on everyone he met, providing spiritual guidance, inspiring the faithful, and turning skeptics to faith. Against an emperor's political ambitions, his orthodox ideas won the day and his teaching shaped the church. Writing in a "festal letter," an annual correspondence ensuring that his African community operated with a common schedule for holy days like Lent and Easter, and addressing matters of general interest, Athanasius lists the books he believes make up the New Testament: "In these [27 writings] alone the teaching of godliness is proclaimed," he wrote. "No one may add to them, and nothing may be taken away from them." A wide variety of lists had been proposed and many would be proposed later. But it was Athanasius's list that the church eventually adopted and the one we still use today.[8]

In a letter of spiritual counsel written to a close friend, this godly African bishop strongly encouraged him to use the psalms: "All Scripture, my son, both ancient and new, is inspired by God and profitable for teaching, as it is written. But the book of Psalms possesses a certain winning exactitude for those who are prayerful." In his letter Athanasius outlines a sort of ancient psalm index or catalog, prescribing particular psalms for particular moods, seasons, and spiritual ailments:

> Another time, perhaps, you find you have been led astray by others' arguments—well, then, the moment you perceive it, stop your sinning, sit down and weep, as they did of old by Babylon's waters, using the words of Psalm 137. . . . For prayer and supplication, sing Psalms 5, 141 to 143, and 146. Has some Goliath risen up against the people and yourself? Fear not, but trust in God, as David did, and sing his words in Psalm 144. . . . If, weak as you are, you yet are chosen for some position of authority among the brethren, you must not be puffed up

as though you were superior to them, but rather glorify the Lord Who chose you and sing Psalm 151, which is especially the Psalm of David. . . .[9]

Especially the psalm of David? Athanasius's reputation for articulating, practicing, and suffering for orthodoxy is legendary. His endorsement of Psalm 151 adds to its credibility, but how is it *especially* the psalm of David?

Like Psalm 151, many psalms include superscriptions. Some of these introductory sentences offer musical direction, pointing psalm readers to particular instruments or a particular tune. For example, Psalm 4 begins, "For the director of music. With stringed instruments." Psalm 5 is "For the director of music. For pipes." Other superscripts place the psalm in an original story. Psalm 3 is prefaced with "A psalm of David. When he fled from Absalom." Psalm 51 begins, "When the prophet Nathan came to him after David had committed adultery with Bathsheba." Thirteen psalms point to a specific story in David's life, many of which are taken directly from the books of 1 and 2 Samuel. Psalm scholars differ on the reliability of these superscripts. Some assume that superscripts are attempts by editors to fit the psalm into specific episodes in David's story since they do not easily match the assigned incident and appear unreliable.

Questions also arise about the authorship of the psalms. Many claim to be "of David"; generations of believers called the entire Psalter "the David." Charles Spurgeon called his book on the psalms *The Treasury of David*. But other psalms claim to be "Of Asaph" or the "Sons of Korah" or even Solomon. Complicating matters more, some psalms seem to be altered slightly by an editor unknown to us.

Psalms 9 and 10 were sometimes used as one psalm, as suggested by their sequence of lines beginning with successive
letters of the Hebrew alphabet. In the same way, Psalms
42 and 43 were once a single psalm but now appear sepa-
rately. Clearly the Qumran community was not the only
group who was editing and compiling the psalms. Centuries
before, possibly in the time of Solomon's temple, there was
likely an original collection of "David's psalms," a compilation that was edited by generations that followed. What
did Athanasius see in Psalm 151 that made this legend of
orthodoxy call it a psalm of David?

A reading of the psalm itself, unfamiliar to many,
may help us understand. The psalm comes to us in two
forms, the first translated from a manuscript found in a
Qumran cave:

> Hallelujah! A psalm of David, son of Jesse. I was
> smaller than my brothers, youngest of my father's
> sons. So he made me a shepherd for his sheep, a
> ruler over his goats. My hands fashioned a pipe,
> my fingers a lyre, and I glorified the Lord. I said to
> myself, "The mountains do not testify to Him, nor
> do the hills proclaim." So echo my words, O trees,
> O sheep, my deeds! Ah, but who can proclaim,
> who declare the deeds of the Lord? God has seen
> all, heard and attended to everything. He sent his
> prophet to anoint me, even Samuel, to raise me up.
> My brothers went forth to meet him: handsome of
> figure, wondrous of appearance, tall were they of
> stature, so beautiful their hair—yet the Lord God
> did not choose them. No, He sent and took me
> who followed the flock, and anointed me with the

holy oil. . . . Then I s[a]w the Philistine, throwing
out taunts from the [enemy] r[anks].[10]

A second version of Psalm 151, as translated in the New
Revised Standard Version, is ascribed to David as his own
composition after he had fought in single combat with
Goliath. It reads,

I was small among my brothers, and the youngest
in my father's house; I tended my father's sheep.
My hands made a harp; my fingers fashioned a lyre.
And who will tell my Lord? The Lord himself; it
is he who hears. It was he who sent his messenger
and took me from my father's sheep, and anointed
me with his anointing-oil. My brothers were handsome and tall, but the Lord was not pleased with
them. I went out to meet the Philistine, and he
cursed me by his idols. But I drew his own sword;
I beheaded him, and took away disgrace from the
people of Israel.

These two versions read like two separate but related
drafts of the same work. That's often the way songwriters
work, writing draft after draft until the work reaches its
final form. A few songs seem born in their final form, as if
dictated directly from heaven: Handel wrote his *Messiah*
almost in a single stream of thought. But most songs take
writing and rewriting, refining and editing. The intricacies
of Psalm 119, for example, must have taken multiple drafts
and multiple editors. The Bible is inspired, but the way
that inspiration happened is mysterious to us. Did Psalm
23 come to David all at once, or did he write in fits and
starts over a single winter of shepherding—or even several
winters? Suppose a fellow shepherd heard David sing an

early version of Psalm 23 while they shared a campfire one evening. And suppose that after parting ways, this friend sang it himself, finding it comforting, and teaching it to other shepherd friends over the months, only to discover later that winter that David had adapted a few of the lines. Without the printed page, it's especially easy to imagine songs or poems in different versions being made and remade, edited and adjusted to fit the pipes or strings or the musicians available on any given day.

My aim is not to build a case to expand the Psalter by one or more psalms or to hunt for the next divinely inspired prayer. But in celebrating the discovery of this one hidden treasure, we can open ourselves more fully to the ongoing creative work of the psalms and follow the Psalter's own instruction to "sing a new song to the LORD." The psalms are always alive, always moving; the spirit of the psalms continues to inspire originality. Generations have prayed the psalms as a sort of launching pad for their own original renditions, sometimes using scraps or sections of the psalms, other times repeating them as a whole.

Isaac Watts, inspired by Psalm 98, wrote the Christmas classic "Joy to the World." His adaptation of Psalm 90," O God Our Help in Ages Past," is often used at state funerals, including that of Winston Churchill in St. Paul's Cathedral in 1965. Martin Luther used Psalm 46 as inspiration for his majestic hymn, "A Mighty Fortress Is Our God," as did the unknown writer of "How Firm a Foundation," a favorite hymn of President Andrew Jackson, who asked for it to be sung at his bedside shortly before he died, and Confederate General Robert E. Lee, who requested it be sung at his funeral. Sir Robert Grant, inspired by William Kethe's translation of Psalm 104 from a 1561 psalm book, wrote the beloved hymn "O Worship the King All Glorious Above."

Psalm 151 was well used and well loved by those living near the caves of Qumran, by a most revered African bishop, and by the writers of the television series *Touched by an Angel*. The protagonist of this faith-based drama is Monica, an angel recently promoted to case work from her original vocation of search and rescue. Posing in human form, she quickly befriends people who are experiencing emotional turmoil, offering them shelter and guidance. In most episodes, Monica ultimately reveals that she is an angel to awaken her subjects to God's deep love for them. Monica's supervisor, Tess, regularly provides her (and indirectly the viewers) with insight into God's ways and plans. A third angel, Andrew, the Angel of Death, supplements his duties as Escort of the Deceased by moonlighting in occasional case work.

The show's one-hundredth episode begins with all three angels in a park celebrating the completion of Monica's one hundredth assignment. Nearby Audrey, a single mother who writes commercial jingles for a living, is celebrating her son Petey's birthday. Attempting to blow out his birthday candles, Petey is overcome by a coughing fit fueled by cystic fibrosis. Later that day, Monica arrives at Petey's home posing as a potential border. Once in residence, she attends Petey's needs. When they discover that Petey doesn't have long to live, Petey and Monica compile a list of the things he wants to do before he dies—learn to play the piano; find a home for Fluffy, his pet iguana; find someone to sing with Mom; and find someone to shovel the snow.

Audrey discovers Petey's list, including his hope that she would complete the song she began at his birth. Audrey tries, but breaks down in tears, unable to get past the first verse. At that point Monica reveals her identity as an angel and encourages her to use this song to tell the world about Petey's love. Working all night to finish, Audrey wakes Petey up in the morning, telling him to cross that item off his list. Petey is taken outdoors to find his neighbors gathered to perform Audrey's now-finished song. She calls it "The 151st Psalm." As his friends sing, Petey tells Andrew, "It is finished," and the young boy dies. It's then that Monica crosses the final item off of Petey's list: "Go to Heaven."[11]

Is this a far-fetched and sentimental example of a television program that works our emotions in the guise of spirituality? Or is it a classic example of an apocryphal psalm inspiring an apocryphal story? Even if the show's writers didn't intend it that way, *Touched by an Angel* shows what the Qumran community knew, what Athanasius knew, what every psalm lover knows—that the psalms are always original and often inspire originality. Sometimes they offer tried and tested words that become our own, other times they inspire us to write an original song or offer a custom prayer in a world of spurious and doubtful circumstances. In a real sense, the Psalter is never complete. Our stories, our pain, our celebrations, and even our apocryphal circumstances join the stories of a thousand generations. The psalms and stories of David and Asaph, of Moses and Solomon, of Athanasius and Petey invite us to view and tell our story as part of God's ongoing work in our less-than-perfectly-ordered world.

A deep love for the canonical psalms inspired the Qumran community to write their own original works, what archeologists now call the Thanksgiving Hymns.

Twenty-five were found on a single manuscript in Cave 1. Each begins with a phrase like "I thank you, Lord" and then voices the present and particular feelings, opinions, and beliefs of their community. Drawing from well-known and well-loved biblical psalms, they created something fresh and deeply personal. One example is what archeologists call "Hymn 9":

> I thank you, Lord (Psalm 57:9) that you have not abandoned me while I sojourn among a (foreign?) people, (and not) according to my guilt have you judged me, nor have you abandoned me among the designs of my inclination, but you have helped my life from the Pit (Jonah 2:6) and you have given (your servant deliverance) in the midst of lions destined for the children of guilt (Psalm 57:4). . . .[12]

In this one hymn the Qumran author makes twenty-nine references to the psalms. "Here then," summarizes Holladay, "is a body of hymns whose writer had drunk deep from all the poetry of Scripture, but most particularly from the Psalms."[13] Ancient words give rise to new original words.

My friend David lives in an area of our city that long-term locals call "Gardenland." Local police officers call it "Heroin Alley." Sociologists call it "the corridor of neglect." David and his family call it home. To understand his new community when he first moved to town, he took a job as a pizza delivery man, joined a soccer league, and served the local high school as a substitute teacher. He wanted to love and serve people in this often overlooked and under-appreciated Hispanic neighborhood. After eight years of tremendous investment by David, his family, and their stalwart band of dedicated Jesus-followers, their average Sunday attendance is twenty-eight. Last week their number was reduced by one.

Gil was David's hero, his friend, confidant, and inspiration. Gil knew the world was broken. He knew that fixing it was beyond his means. But instead of retreating to the sidelines in despair, he boldly entered into the pain around him. He felt strong anger at injustice: Why do all the new businesses, city services, and churches go to the new section of town, ignoring us? But even in the middle of such lament, Gil's face and actions shone with unmistakable joy. Gil was lying in bed, sick and fading, the Sunday before he died, when David read to him from Psalm 4:

Answer me when I call to you, my righteous God. Give me relief from my distress; have mercy on me and hear my prayer. How long will you people turn my glory into shame? How long will you love delusions and seek false gods? . . . Many, LORD, are asking, "Who will bring us prosperity?" Let the light of your face shine on us. Fill my heart with joy when their grain and new wine abound. In peace I will lie down and sleep, for you alone, LORD, make me dwell in safety.

Following Gil's death, David wrote an email to friends that was part blog, part elegy, and part prayer. He began by quoting from Psalm 4, and then, as if launched into remembering, he said, "Gil was the first person I met in Sacramento. He excitedly told me about the history, the diversity, the troubles, and the amazing families of his neighborhood. He said that they were feeling left behind;

that the energy and interest, the parks and the money, were skipping over older neighborhoods and going only to the new." Gil, he said, knew that all people, even those in forgotten neighborhoods, have inherent dignity and resourcefulness; that dignity comes not from accumulating money or achieving education or political power, but from our status as imagebearers of God. Then, much like the Thanksgiving Hymns of the Qumran community, David's psalm-inspired reflection shifted into obvious prayer: "Let us see the brokenness all around us and care enough to get to work, so 'his kingdom may come on earth as it is in heaven.' God, open my eyes, my heart, and my hands. God, help my life to inspire others to do the same. Give us friends to do the same." In the spirit of the Qumran author, of Isaac Watts, Martin Luther, and Sir Robert Grant, this modern David wrote his own hymn, an original prayer inspired by the original Psalm 4.

Eelco Vos puts the same originality into his music. On his fifth birthday, Eelco received an undersized psalm song-book from his grandfather, a book of melodies and metrical (rhyming) translations of the psalms dating back to the 1500s. Still sung throughout the world, its original vision was inspired by Geneva's most famous pastor, John Calvin, who longed to enable faithful believers to sing God's own prayers in their own language—a strikingly novel idea at the time. Calvin commissioned writers and composers, who worked for over twenty years to compose the Genevan Psalter, the original version of the palm-size book Vos had received from his grandfather.

Eelco inherited this psalm-singing tradition with little enthusiasm. As a child, he says, its 450-year-old magic was lost on him. Far from dazzled, he experienced the book as an unappealing frustration, magnified because he was forced to regularly memorize its lines. The psalms seemed distant and insulated, far removed from the vigor and pain of real life.

But as an adult Eelco's feelings shifted. He found himself so treasuring the oft-sung melodies that he determined to preserve and invigorate them, even to invite new participants into the Psalter's riches. These days he composes up-to-date arrangements, combining his skills as a pianist and composer with the artistry of friends playing cello, flute, and guitar. Inspired by his infatuation with the psalms, the vintage melodies and texts are awakened to new life. Now his tunes are inspiring a new generation of psalm singers—he calls them "new shoots from our spiritual and cultural roots."[14]

Ken Medema had his own reasons for dodging the psalms. A child of devout parents, he was eight years old when someone asked his parents to store a piano for them. After a few weeks of listening to his unending banging, they decided he needed lessons. They found a piano teacher Ken describes as a wonder. Soon she was teaching him music history, music theory, and a wide range of styles. She read him excerpts from Plato, Alfred North Whitehead, and Sartre, inspiring in him an intellectual restlessness that led him to declare himself an agnostic in the tenth grade.

It wasn't until he met a Baptist minister's daughter during his university days that Ken reexamined his faith. An outrageously good musician, wonderful pianist, and thoughtful person, she was unfazed by his questions, and even shared some of them. Ken had always assumed that Christians didn't ask questions about who God is, but she disagreed. "Christians doubt like everyone else does," she insisted. Ken remembers, "As I sat in her home listening to her family's conversations, I realized they were asking the same questions I was. The only difference was that they were asking the questions from inside their faith. Questions were not a threat, but theological play. You could ask all the questions you wanted and have many remain unanswered, but in the end trust trumps certitude every time. Their attitude brought me back to faith." Gradually he started attending church again with his reflective friend, who eventually became his wife.[15]

The psalms Medema sang as a churchgoing child never left him. Years after reentering the church, Medema was invited to be the featured musician at a gathering of three thousand Christian teens. It was the 1970s, and the charismatic renewal movement was sweeping the church. TV evangelists were everywhere, he remembers. Convention planners chose the theme "Thriving in the Spirit." Asked to write a new song for those spiritually-charged days, Medema took one look at the convention logo, a flourishing tree, and decided, "This church loves the psalms, and Psalm 1 is about a tree. I'm going to take off on that." He knew that teens in the 70s couldn't imagine any psalm being hip, but he wanted to tap into their buried roots and "bring them back to their identity." The result was a fresh version of Psalm 1 he named "The Tree Song"—a song that endures.[16]

Like the Qumran cave dwellers of long ago, Medema, inspired by the canonical psalms, began to compose new, original versions. But it wasn't until he was invited to join a small group that was compiling a new songbook made entirely of psalms[17] that Medema fully grasped the level of storytelling imbedded in the psalms or their reservoir of emotion, of debate and conflict and questions and wondering. Suddenly, he says, the psalms took on a whole new life.

This gathering of Bible scholars and musicians was unlike anything he had experienced. Together they sought what Medema calls "the turn"—the moment the psalm's storyline shifts and its emotions change. He was recruited to use their collective study of a psalm's particular structure to score original music. Despite his intuitive storytelling skills, Medema had never considered using the psalm's own storyline to write a song.

That first afternoon the group worked on Psalm 73. It begins with a complaint: Why are evil people flourishing while the godly flounder? As Ken reflected on the psalmist's experience an old Carter family song from the 1960s sprang to mind—"It takes a worried man to sing a worried song . . . I'm worried now, but I won't be worried long. . . ." He thought he'd found the perfect song to communicate the emotions of this psalm. Then, he says, came "the turn" where the psalm writer says, "I was all goofed up about how well the wicked were doing. I tried to walk the way of God, but walking with God got me nowhere. Until I came into the sanctuary, and that's when my eyes were opened." To help a new generation of singers follow the psalm's emotional shift, Medema altered the entire feel and texture of the music. "Until I came into your presence, O God, my eyes were opened and my vision was clear. The life I envied is a castle of sand, falling to nothing when a strong wind comes near." The psalmist, says Medema, saw that the life he wanted was ephemeral; it meant nothing. Medema's new song followed the psalm's resolution: "My life turned upside-down and now I can see there is a treasure that will not fade away. You draw me near to you, O God. You hold me in your hand. . . ."[18] It is, says Medema, the chorale at end of the cantata. It's the resolution that goes back into major chords, providing the story's finale. On hearing Medema's rendition of their Psalm 73 reflections, the group responded, "That's what we've been talking about!"

Of course, Medema has a rare gift. He's a stellar songwriter described by one admiring musician as "able to harvest an entire field from the tiniest seed of composition, and on the spot at that." Another musician notes his uncanny vision and a remarkable skill for putting the ideas of Scripture and song together.

Months later the small group who first heard Medema's song based on Psalm 73 grew to a summer gathering of fifty psalm enthusiasts, lyricists, and composers. Together they explored music styles ranging from "dub"—a kind of calypso forerunner to hip-hop—to African-American, Latin, and global influences. Once again Medema worked his artistry. In the middle of a wide-ranging discussion about a particular psalm he would spontaneously start to sing an original on-the-spot composition. One musician jumped up to grab his string bass, another grabbed his guitar. Both cocked their heads listening for the chords being played. Together they started jamming, and attendees soon started singing along in a room lit up by their smiles.

Of course not everyone is a songwriter like Eelco Vos or Ken Medema. Not everyone writes original prayers like the Sons of Zadok, or elegies like my friend David. And very few people are lucky enough to discover hidden treasure in a cave. But might it be that if we listen to the music in our head and the words in our heart we'll discover that we each have our own custom psalm to sing? Our very own Psalm 151? Or 152?

EPILOGUE

Finding Your Place

"*Nowhere can we be more certain that we are praying with the Holy Spirit than when we pray the psalms.*"[1]

—Thomas Merton

"*It is therefore easy to understand why the Book of Psalms is the favorite book of all the saints. For every man on every occasion can find in it Psalms which fit his needs, which he feels to be as appropriate as if they had been set there just for his sake.*"[2]

—Martin Luther

This is a book of stories. Each serves as a kind of introduction, an overture to make the psalms' messy, confusing, rousing, and inspiring brand of prayer our own. Each story is a kind of friend, a host who invites us into a new and deeper level of friendship with God, one that is more frank and guileless, more bracing and invigorating than we thought possible.

In that spirit, let me close with two more.

The call came on my day off. The past weeks had been a blur. Christmas was barely past. A tantalizing job opportunity was coaxing me away from our much-loved congregation. Days filled with intense family conversations around the possibility of moving adolescent children cross country. My previous day off had included an extended conversation with the search committee. The following weekend I would be on site for a visit.

The call came from a former church staff member who had my cell phone number. My frayed emotions staggered at the sound of the phone. Couldn't it wait? My reaction signaled inner spiritual malaise and a flunking grade at clergy balance.

I listened to my friend's message. "I'm so sorry to bother you on your day off," she began. I found myself thinking, *This had better be good.* "But my friend's three-month-old granddaughter died last night. They don't know what to do. They don't have a church. Is there any chance you could visit them, even on your day off?" In the face of that family's plight even my drained spiritual gas tank found a few drops of compassion to stoke my pastoral engine. These are holy moments—times it is an honor to be in ministry. "I'll be right there," I said.

Driving toward their home, I found myself asking the ageless pastoral question "What do you say at a time like this?" From a previous conversation I knew that this young grandmother had had a ghastly upbringing. The sinister suffering she had experienced as a child would make the most pious saint question God's existence, let alone God's character. Despite her past she turned to God occasionally, even if she shied away from church.

What *do* you say? What does anyone say in the face of such grief? How do you begin to find words to speak to a family who had lost their child and grandchild hours before? What seminary education, what therapeutic training gives you wisdom for such a loss?

I remembered the first time I was called to such a crisis. A rookie pastor in small-town Minnesota, I'd signed up for a weekly shift as a volunteer hospital chaplain. One of my first weeks on the job, a hospital administrator phoned unexpectedly. "Would you come to the hospital? A couple just gave birth to their first child and it's stillborn. They're holding him in their arms. They need someone to talk to." Childless ourselves, my wife and I had recently experienced our third miscarriage. But they were experiencing a different sort of grief. What do you pray? Twenty years after that hospital visit my question hadn't changed.

Greeting me at the door, my friend led me inside, where the family was scattered throughout the house. Unable to sit still, the jittery, twenty-something father bounced between rooms working his cell phone. Calling friends and family, he tried to answer the unanswerable— what happened? His girlfriend, the grieving mother, was in despair. Looking from her mom and back to me, she searched our faces. What did I do wrong? What did I do to deserve this? She replayed the conversations of her nightmare morning. Yesterday her darling daughter had been perfectly healthy. But at the time of her pre-dawn feeding she was still, a sight that will forever haunt the young mother's dreams. They called 911. Firefighters charged to their home and tried to resuscitate her. EMT personnel raced in behind them. Moments later police arrived, sealing off the bedroom as a possible crime scene. Each team of rescuers came to help, but they also came with a barrage of questions that felt like an interrogation to this stunned young couple.

We sat around the kitchen table: anguished young mother, grieving grandmother, loyal friend, and unknown pastor. Empty beverage containers lined the counter like disorganized centerpieces. The grieving step-granddad rotated between sitting on the couch to listen and stepping outside for a smoke. What do you say?

"Would you tell me about your daughter?" The question seemed to refocus her angst. A litany of delights poured out: her favorite words and phrases, her winning smile and laugh. But even holy remembering didn't bury her questions. She asked again, "What did I do wrong?" Biblically unschooled, she frantically searched her smorgasbord of spiritual understanding for something to bring comfort in her most painful hour. "Maybe God made her an angel because he wanted her to fly around sharing her joy with more people?" She looked at Grandma who, I was relieved to see, remained unconvinced. She tried again, "Maybe God took her to help Jesus save people?" Again, her mom refused to feed her spiritual speculation. Then guilt gushed out: "Every night I prayed with her 'Now I lay me down to sleep I pray the Lord my soul to keep.' But last night we were rushed. It was the only time I didn't pray those words. Is it my fault she died?" Our quick and collective no was deep enough to fend off more superstitious suspicions.

After a time, I sensed the conversation winding to a close. Nothing was fixed; my presence hadn't worked any miracles. But after twenty years a pastor knows when it's time to move on. In the religiously oriented subculture of Minnesota such moments called for an ancient pastoral liturgy familiar to church-attending and church-avoiding people alike. Even rookie pastors knew the rhythm: conversation followed by Bible reading and prayer. But here in the religiously adverse suburbs of California, in the presence of restless, irreligious folks, that old-time liturgy seemed out of place.

I wondered if there might be a way to get the jittery dad and chain-smoking step-granddad to join our conversation. What would be meaningful to people several steps removed from organized religion? I offered a suggestion, "Would it be OK if we hold hands and pray? I'd like to lead us in Psalm 23. It's a time-tested prayer to use when people don't know what to say. If you know it, you can say it too. If not, it's OK." So in that circle of grief I prayed those familiar, iconic words. Together we prayed toward green pastures and through the "valley of shadow of death." We prayed to "dwell in the house of the Lord forever." And when the psalm ended we went on praying. I thanked God for the gift of their daughter. I asked God to help those young parents love each other in the middle of tragedy. I thanked him for friends and prayed for the grandparents. And then we said Amen.

After parting handshakes to the father and hugs to the mom and grandma I walked to the door. The step-granddad had disappeared, and I found myself wondering if I had misjudged the situation. Was I being too religious? But as I pulled the front door open to leave, the step-granddad rushed toward me. With tears in his eyes he pumped my hand. "Thank you," he kept saying. Then he hugged me.[3]

Prayer can be informed by all kinds of wisdom. Some wisdom comes from a therapeutic framework and is gleaned from decades of counseling. Some comes from theological knowledge based on piecing together contours of the afterlife, the full effects of Jesus' resurrection. In that moment, inspired by the stories of those who have gone before, I was able to point this shaken family to the psalmist's ancient, proven words. Knowing a psalm helped us to dodge the pious clichés that are the favorites of a religious subculture. The psalms' timeless vocabulary offers spiritual novices and longtime believers comfort none of us can find in any other place.

That was two years ago. I'd like to report that the grieving family is now safe in the womb of the church, flourishing members of a community that loves and sustains them. I'd like to report that this first psalm conversation led to another, and that these ancient words led the family to an earthy, robust, girder-strong spiritual faith. I'd like to report that. But it wouldn't be the truth.

As a group, they are still suspicious of the church. They still hang in a sort of relational suspension, hovering in orbit around our congregation. They know where we are and some of the people who attend. But they keep their distance. Still, their reaction that morning helps me believe again in the power of the psalms to provide a kind of scaffolding that can help hold even the most tottering faith in place.

A year after that impromptu visit, I made another visit. John and Nancy[4] started coming to our church the day our building opened. Classy and well-styled, Nancy always walked in behind Johnny, dressed in flannel shirts and comfortable clothes. Every week she followed him, smiling and pushing his wheelchair. John and I teased each other often. I'd tease him about his caregiver—"If she ever gives you any trouble, you call the church." He wasn't able to form words, but he laughed at even my sorriest jokes.

Several months after their first visit Nancy made an appointment to visit me at my office. Johnny was a good man, she said. A hard worker. A Korean war veteran. They'd been married over forty years. But after his stroke several years earlier, he refused to accept anyone's help but Nancy's. So she cared for him: fed him, bathed him, loved him, and brought him to church. Now she had to tell me that she was wearing out. Long past being tired, she was exhausted, and she didn't know how long she could endure. I empathized and listened. Together we brainstormed options. Might some guys from church be able to watch him while she went to Bible study? Could some of us help get him and his wheelchair into their car for a dinner out? We laughed and cried and prayed together. None of our plans worked. But Nancy kept on feeding and bathing and loving and shuttling John around.

Five years later on a Sunday morning firefighters arrived at their home. John had fallen and Nancy couldn't lift him back up. After trying for what seemed like an eternity, not knowing what else to do, she called 911. Soon some of our city's finest, strong firefighters in leather boots and blue uniforms, rushed to her aid. They propped John on the family couch. And that's where he was when I came after the morning services. John sat on the couch unclothed. A blanket was draped over his shoulders but succumbing to gravity. Nancy, the epitome of composure and wifely strength, said with exhausted desperation, "I don't know how much longer I can take this." Months had worn into years. Each new day was harder than the one before.

As we talked together, Sidney and Sophie, their two Havanese dogs, barked a high-decibel warning. Penned behind a makeshift barrier on the other side of the room, they did everything they could to diffuse our poignant conversation. I'm used to the clutter backdrop for ministry. But these dogs were hard to ignore.

Nancy relayed the morning's drama. We caught up on the details of the past week. And then we turned our attention again to John. We talked about his good life. We talked about his long courageous battle, living with the aftermath of a stroke. And we talked about his impending death. Especially we talked about the valley of the shadow of death. I assured him that there is a shepherd who has already gone through that valley and who came back. "When your time comes, John," I said, "he will guide you through that valley. He's been through it before, and he knows how to guide you home. You can trust him." I say *we* talked—but actually I talked. And John nodded. A couple of times he nodded off—part of the noxious power of his stroke. All the while Nancy listened, worn and anxious and concerned for her longtime spouse.

Then I asked the pastor question: "Can we pray together?" John sat semi-clothed on the couch, Nancy in a chair, and I scooted temporarily in front of their coffee table. We held hands, a ritual of sorts, and prayed. I began with the familiar words "The Lord is my shepherd, I shall not want." All the while the dogs kept barking their high-pitched diversion. But my mind was registering, it seemed, another noise. I kept going, "He makes me lie down in green pastures, he leads me beside quiet waters . . ." Then I realized that John was praying the psalm with me. In that moment his memory tamed his stroke-damaged brain cells. His words were garbled, but I knew what he was praying. Nancy knew what he was praying. Most importantly, John knew what he was praying. I started to cry. I couldn't go on. I was overwhelmed. This man, who couldn't speak or hold himself up or stay awake during a brief conversation, could say this psalm. From memory.

But now I, the veteran pastor, was messing up his recall, ruining a poignant moment. Emotionally overcome, I had lost my place. "Can we start over?" I asked. John nodded. And so we did. This time we prayed together, past the "quiet waters" and the "presence of my enemies," all the way to "Surely goodness and mercy will follow me all the days of my life, and I will dwell in the house of the Lord forever." Johnny prayed all the way to the end. I was still crying. The dogs were still barking. Not exactly a Hallmark moment, but a heavenly one. I'm sure God was praying with us.

The psalms are not magic formulas or silver bullets. They are not lucky charms, spiritual talismans, or pious clichés. They are prayers. A very special kind of prayer. The kind that helps a stroke victim and his spouse pray when they have run out of strength; the kind that offers words to comfort a biblically inexperienced family pray in their darkest moment; the kind that gives us words to express our own grief and longing, revenge or joy. No wonder generations of parents have taught the psalms to their children. No wonder centuries of ministry leaders consider the psalms essential tools for their ministry. No wonder that in the ancient church it was not unusual to memorize "the entire David." In the words of Psalm 119, the psalms make us wiser than our teachers (v. 99).

My friend, the one who disturbed my day off not long ago, wrote me later that day. Her own journey of faith is new and often puzzling. But that day among her hurting friends she was the veteran believer. She had something to offer, something helpful. "I'm filled with hope," she wrote. "It's hard to turn away and question this mysterious God when he presents himself to you in the form of a pastor who speeds to sit with a young mother and her family who have lost a child . . . who doesn't turn away at their swear words . . . who doesn't judge . . . who is filled with grace in a time of need. Thank you for opening that door for them."

I tell these stories so you can add your own. So you can join my friend; and Ambrose, who called the psalms "a kind of play"; and John and Nancy, who prayed through his final hours together; and John Calvin, who called the Psalter "an anatomy of all the parts of the soul"; and an Eritrean refugee who protected her preschool children from bullets; and Dietrich Bonhoeffer, who said that in the psalms "we learn to speak to God because God has spoken and speaks to us." These stories, of course, are barely a beginning. Just enough to help us see how our story (and our prayer) is already part of God's timeless community. As we voice to God our unvarnished prayers, we already belong.

ACKNOWLEDGMENTS

"No books of moral tales and no legends of saints which have been written or ever will be written are to my mind as noble as the Book of Psalms...."[1]

—Martin Luther

During grade school my two younger brothers and I would occasionally stay overnight at Grandma's house. Each stay was a mighty big event for us, and now I'm sure, for my parents, who must have eagerly welcomed a break from parenting three boys. Grandma didn't drive, but we'd take the city bus downtown, eat a "burger basket," visit the museum, and return home to play rousing games of dominoes and Parcheesi. She'd spoil us with Faygo Red Pop and homemade cookies, and eventually send us to bed upstairs.

During one stay I awoke earlier than my brothers and descended the stairs. I must have been especially quiet because I found Grandma in her rocking chair, gazing out her favorite window. A Dutch version of the Genevan Psalter was in her lap, and she was singing softly. Decades later I still remember the serene look on her face. As far as I can remember, no one in my church or family told me I ought to pray; they simply did so, and expected their faith to take hold in me. I'm grateful it did. In their praying and singing, I met Jesus. And so I owe Grandma and the rest of my family a great debt.

In writing this book I owe more thanks than I can say, but let me acknowledge some:

To the people of Granite Springs Church: I consider myself most fortunate to belong to a congregation that loves and lives grace. Every day you offer people space to bring their faith and doubt. You dared explore the psalms (another crazy idea from your pastor) for an entire year in sermons, small groups, and conversations. Thank you for trusting me with your stories, and for writing new ones together. You teach me about faith every day.

To Len Vander Zee, a superb editor who took a chance on an inexperienced author, refining the original idea and greatly improving this project with insightful suggestions.

To everyone at Square Inch Publishing for making this book a reality.

To John Witvliet, Neal Plantinga, and Dale Cooper, whose conversations in the early stages of this project offered strategic encouragement and wisdom to get me started.

To the staff of the Calvin Institute for Christian Worship: these words are the fruit of your stellar work and love for congregations.

To Emily Brink, Ken Medema, and Carl Bosma, who each took extra time to tell me their own psalm stories.

To Tim Brown, who I heard so wisely chant as a refrain, "The human heart is too thin a platform on which to build a prayer life, so God has given us a book. . . ."

To the staff of Granite Springs Church: thanks for being comrades-in-arms on the walk of faith. It is a privilege to work shoulder to shoulder with you, spreading grace.

To all those who have written on the psalms before me: I have done my best to give you all the credit you deserve, but my debt to you is immense, and in many cases it is impossible to untangle your thinking from my own.

To Mom and Dad: I owe you more than I can say.

To Gerry, Luke, Rachel, and JJ, who bore with the entire process of writing, often enduring my neglect while I holed myself up with the manuscript, which became a sort of temporary and demanding additional family member: you make my heart sing.

Share your own psalm story and read
others online at www.psalmstory.com.

NOTES

Introduction

1. Letter of Athanasius, Archbishop of Alexandria, to Marcellinus.
2. Martin Luther, quoted in Dietrich Bonhoeffer, *Psalms: The Prayer Book of the Bible* (Minneapolis: Augsburg Fortress, 1970), p. 25.
3. From "Science, Faith, and Survival: Conversation with Natan Sharansky" by Harry Kreisler. 4/16/04. Conversations with History; Institute of International Studies, UC Berkeley. http://globetrotter.berkeley.edu/people4/Sharansky/sharansky-con3.html.
4. Alicia Ostriker, "Psalm and Anti-Psalm: A Personal Interlude" in *Poets on the Psalms* (San Antonio: Trinity University Press, 2008), p. 20.
5. From "Words for the Heart." Transcript of a conversation between David Gergen and Peter Gomes, December 25, 1996. http://www.pbs.org/newshour/gergen/december96/gomes_12-24.html.
6. Jewel, quoted in David Goetz, "Suburban Spirituality," *Christianity Today*, July 2003.
7. C. S. Lewis. *Reflections on the Psalms* (New York: Harcourt Brace Jovanovich), p. 75.

Chapter 1

1. Immanuel Kant, from a letter to Heinrich Stilling, quoted in Martin Hoag, *He Is Our Life* (Stuttgart: JF Steinkopf Verlag, 1952), p. 209.
2. William L. Holladay, *The Psalms through Three Thousand Years* (Minneapolis: Fortress Press, 1996), p. 361. I am

indebted to Holladay for this story and several others in this chapter.

3. Ibid., p. 359.

4. Ibid., p. 364.

5. Taken from "Jesus Walks," written by Kanye West and Rhymefest, recorded on *The College Dropout,* © 2004, Roc-A-Fella Records, LLC (a division of Def Jam recordings and Universal Music Publishing Group). Used by permission.

6. Karl Jacobson, "Through the Pistol Smoke Dimly: Psalm 23 in Contemporary Film and Song," Society of Biblical Literature. http://sbl-site.org/publications/article.aspx?articleId=796.

7. Harold W. Attridge and Margot E. Fassler, eds., *Psalms in Community: Jewish and Christian Textual, Liturgical, and Artistic Traditions* (Atlanta: Society of Biblical Literature, 2003), p. 397.

8. Abraham Joshua Heschel, *The Sabbath* (New York: Farrar, Straus and Giroux, 1951, 1979), p. 13.

9. More and more scholars view Psalm 23 as part of a collection of psalms—a mini-Psalter within the Psalter. Psalms 15 and 24, emphasizing God's high majesty and his insistence on a life of moral purity, frame this collection. Psalm 19, a poetic masterpiece highlighting human delight in God's created world and in his life-giving Torah, sits strategically in the album's center. Each remaining psalm has a twin. So Psalm 16, which begins, "Keep me safe, my God for in you I take refuge" pairs with Psalm 23, "The Lord is my shepherd." The two psalms share multiple themes, including the threat of death. And in a cluster of psalms that

prioritizes living God's law, both remind us that trust is essential to obedience. Might knowing this ancient editorial move enable us to better understand this favorite psalm, to help us more clearly see its larger place in the story of God's people, a story bigger and messier and with a stronger call to trust than we imagine?

10. Rodney L. Cooper, "African American Preaching," from PreachingTodaySermons.com.

11. Adapted from Timothy Brown's lecture at Granite Springs Church, January 2009. Used by permission.

Chapter 2

1. C. S. Lewis, *Reflections on the Psalms* (New York: Harcourt Brace Jovanovich), p. 23.

2. This story is adapted from Stephen Tomkins, *John Wesley: A Biography* (Grand Rapids, Mich.: Eerdmans, 2003), pp. 6-7.

3. Ibid., p. 77.

4. Ibid., p. 111

5. John Wesley, from Nehemiah Curnock, ed., *The Journal of the Rev. John Wesley,* 8 volumes. (Whitefish, Mont.: Kessinger Publishing, 2007), vol. 2 pp. 221-22.

6. Eugene H. Peterson, *Answering God: The Psalms as Tools for Prayer* (San Francisco: Harper Collins, 1989), pp. 95-96.

7. Lewis, *Reflections on the Psalms*, p. 21.

8. Ibid.

9. Janet McCann, "Rereading the Psalms," in *Poets on the Psalms* (San Antonio: Trinity University Press, 2008), p. 153.

10. Ibid., pp. 154-55.

11. This prayer is attributed to the theologian Reinhold Niebuhr, who says he wrote the prayer in 1934 for use in a sermon. Niebuhr was quoted in *Grapevine: The International Journal of Alcoholics Anonymous* (January 1950) as saying the prayer "may have been spooking around for years, even centuries, but I don't think so. I honestly do believe that I wrote it myself."

12. Denise Dombkowski Hopkins, *Journey through the Psalms* (St. Louis: Chalice Press, 2002), pp. 87-88.

13. The original setting of many psalms is unknown to us. Such generalities can be helpful; not knowing the specific trouble of the psalmist, we freely insert our own.

14. James Luther Mays, *The Lord Reigns: A Theological Handbook to the Psalms* (Louisville: Westminster John Knox Press, 1994), p. 102.

15. Geffery B. Kelley and F. Burton Nelson, ed. *A Testament to Freedom: The Essential Writings of Dietrich Bonhoeffer* (San Francisco: Harper Collins, 1995), p. 132. The German *dem Rad in die Speichen fallen* is more graphic: "to fall into the spokes of the wheels" implies that protestors throw themselves into the wheel of injustice to clog it and stop it, even at the price of one's life.

16. Eric Metaxas, *Bonhoeffer: Pastor, Martyr, Prophet, Spy, A Righteous Gentile vs. the Third Reich* (Nashville: Thomas Nelson, 2010), p. 368.

17. Ibid.

18. Ibid., p. 358.

19. Letter written on May 15, 1943. From Eberhard Bethge, ed. *Dietrich Bonhoeffer: Letters and Papers from Prison* (New York: Macmillan, 1971) p. 40.

20. Dietrich Bonhoeffer, *Psalms, The Prayer Book of the Bible* (Augsburg Fortress, 1974), p. 26.

21. Metaxas, *Bonhoeffer: Pastor, Martyr, Prophet, Spy,* p. 532.
22. Eric Sarwar, from "Why Persecuted Christians Sing Psalms in Pakistan," Dec 18, 2009. http://worship.calvin.edu/resources.

Chapter 3

1. Basil the Great, *Homilia in psalmum I* quoted in John Witvliet, *The Biblical Psalms in Christian Worship* (Grand Rapids, Mich.: Eerdmans, 2007), p. 4.
2. Collins, Aldrin, and Neal Armstrong quotes from http://history.nasa.gov/SP-350/ch-11-7.html.
3. David McCullough, *Brave Companions: Portraits in History* (New York: Simon & Schuster, 1992), p. 3.
4. Ibid., p. 7.
5. Ibid., p. 18.
6. Ibid., p. 19.
7. Charles Haddon Spurgeon, *The Treasury of David*, quoting Alexander Von Humboldt, 1850.
8. John Moring, *Men with Sand: Great Explorers of the North American West* (Helena: Mont.: Falcon, 1998) p. iii.
9. Ibid.
10. From a television miniseries produced by Steven Spielberg, *Into the West*, 2005.
11. Adam Hochschild, *Bury the Chains: Prophets and Rebels in the Fight to Free an Empire's Slaves* (Boston: Houghton Mifflin, 2005), p. 15.
12. Ibid., pp. 61-67.
13. Theodore Dwight Weld, *The Bible Against Slavery: An Inquiry into the Patriarchal and Mosaic Systems on the Subject of Human Rights.* Classic Reprint Series: Forgotten Books, www.forgottenbooks.org. p. 16.
14. Hochschild, *Bury the Chains*, p. 338.

15. James L. Mays, *Preaching and Teaching the Psalms* (Louisville: Westminster/John Knox, 2006), p. 98.
16. Huxley, quoted in James L. Mays, *Preaching and Teaching the Psalms*, p. 97.

Chapter 4

1. Bono, "Psalm Like It Hot" in *The Guardian* (UK), October 31, 1999, www.atu2.com/news/psalm-like-it-hot.html.
2. John Van Sloten, *The Day Metallica Came to Church: Searching for the Everywhere God in Everything* (Grand Rapids: Square Inch, 2010) p. 34.
3. Ibid., pp. 40-41.
4. Bono, "Psalm Like It Hot."
5. Patrick Henry Reardon, *Christ in the Psalms* (Ben Lomond, Calif.: Conciliar Press, 2000), p. 23.
6. James Luther Mays, *The Lord Reigns: A Theological Handbook to the Psalms* (Louisville: Westminster John Knox, 1994), p. 57.
7. Diet Eman with James Schaap, *Things We Couldn't Say* (Grand Rapids, Mich.: Eerdmans, 1994), p. 364.
8. Van Sloten, *The Day Metallica Came to Church*, pp. 40-47.
9. Ibid., p. 21.

Chapter 5

1. Simone Weil, quoted in Philip Yancey, *Rumors of Another World* (Grand Rapids, Mich. Zondervan, 2003), p. 37.
2. Arnold Dallimore, *Spurgeon* (Chicago: Moody Press, 1984), p. 173.
3. Erroll Hulse and David Kingdon, eds., *A Marvelous Ministry: How the All-round Ministry of Charles Haddon Spurgeon Speaks to Us Today* (Ligonier, Penn.: Soli Deo Gloria Publications, 1993), pp. 35, 69.

4. Charles Spurgeon, *Lectures to My Students* (Grand Rapids, Mich.: Zondervan, 1972), p. 163.

5. John Hellman, *Simone Weil: An Introduction to Her Thought* (Waterloo: Wilfrid Laurier University Press, 1982), p. 48.

6. Simone Weil, *Waiting for God* (New York: Harper Perennial Classics, 2000), p. 27.

7. Simone Weil, *The Notebooks of Simone Weil*, Vol. 2 (London: Routledge & Kegan Paul, 1952-55), p. 449.

8. Leonard Bernstein, quoted in "Leonard Bernstein: A Total Embrace of Music," www.classicalnotes.net/features/bernstein.html.

9. Joseph Pearce, "J. R. R. Tolkien: Truth and Myth," Catholic Education Resources Center, 2001, www.catholiceducation.org.

10. Alan Jacobs, *The Narnian: The Life and Imagination of C. S. Lewis* (New York: HarperCollins, 2005), p. 239.

11. Ibid., p. 297.

12. C. S. Lewis. *Reflections on the Psalms* (New York: Harcourt Brace Jovanovich), p. 46.

13. Ibid., p. 52.

14. Charles Spurgeon, *The Treasury of David.* Completed sections of his commentary on the psalms were released over a twenty-year span until his seventh and final volume was released in 1885. Within ten years more than 120,000 sets had been sold. The work is still available in print from Pilgrim Publishers, Pasadena, Texas, as well as online.

15. Weil, *Waiting for God*, p. 159.

16. Elaine Scarry, *On Beauty and Being Just* (Princeton: Princeton University Press, 1999), p. 112.

17. Walter Brueggemann, The *Message of the Psalms: A Theological Commentary* (Minneapolis: Augsburg, 1985), p. 152.

18. Martin Luther King, Jr. *The Papers of Martin Luther King, Jr.: Advocate of the Social Gospel* (Berkeley, University of California Press, 2007), pp. 226ff.

19. *Ebony*, January 1970. In an interview after King's assassination, Abernathy told *Ebony* magazine that he read Psalm 27 every morning as a way to prepare for the inevitable, his own martyrdom.

20. Edward K. Kaplan, *Spiritual Radical: Abraham Joshua Heschel in America 1940-1972* (New Haven, Yale University Press, 2007), p. 150.

21. Kaplan, *Spiritual Radical*, p. 223.

22. Susanna Heschel, "Following in My Father's Footsteps: Selma 40 years later," *Vox of Darthmouth*, April 4, 2005. www.dartmouth.edu/-vox/0405/0404/heschel.html.

23. Simone Weil, *Letter to a Priest* (New York: Penguin, 2003), p. 11.

Chapter 6

1. Sebastian Moore, quoted in Kathleen Norris, *The Cloister Walk* (New York: Riverhead Books, 1996), p. 91.

2. Ben Patterson, "Schooled by the Psalms," *Christianity Today*, October 2008. www.christianitytoday.com/ct/2008/october/34.87.html.

3. Beth Lantinga, "Holding Fast to the Psalms: Stories from Hungary," *Reformed Worship* 70. www.reformedworship.org.

4. Ibid.

5. Norris, *The Cloister Walk*, pp. 90-91.

6. Ibid., p. xviii

7. Ibid., p. 92

8. Ibid., p. 100
9. Ibid., p. 101
10. Kathleen Norris, "Why the Psalms Scare Us," *Christianity Today*, July 15, 1996. www.christianitytoday. com/ct/1996/july15/6t818b.html.
11. Thomas Merton, *Praying the Psalms* (Collegeville, Minn.: The Liturgical Press, 1956), p. 7.
12. Thomas Merton, *Bread in the Wilderness* (New York: New Directions, 1953), p. 129.
13. Merton, *Praying the Psalms*, p. 8.
14. Merton, *Bread in the Wilderness*, p. 3.
15. Merton, *Praying the Psalms*, pp. 20-21.
16. Ibid., p. 37.
17. Norris, *The Cloister Walk*, p. 107.

Chapter 7

1. James Luther Mays, *The Lord Reigns: A Theological Handbook to the Psalms* (Louisville: Westminster John Knox Press, 1994), p. 42.
2. Michael Perry, *Population 485: Meeting Your Neighbors One Siren at a Time* (New York: Harper Perennial, 2003), p. 153.
3. Ibid., p. 160.
4. Henry Francis Lyte, quoted in "Henry Francis Lyte, 1793-1847," www.stempublishing.com.

Chapter 8

1. Augustine's legacy still casts a long shadow in church teaching and practice. Soon after his death, the church gathered the psalms of his last days, along with a few others (6, 32, 38, 51, 102, and 143), into a collection called *The Seven Penitential Psalms*. Following Augustine's example, medieval monks recited Psalm 130 after lauds

on Fridays during Lent, expressing sorrow for their sin. Orthodox monks still chant it at Tuesday morning vigils, and twice each day for the departed.

2. John Stubbs, *John Donne: The Reformed Soul* (New York: W.W. Norton & Company, 2007), p. 63.

3. Ibid., p. 231.

4. Ibid., p. 330.

5. Evelyn M. Simpson, ed. *John Donne's Sermons on the Psalms: With a Selection of Prayers* (Berkeley: University of California Press, 1963), p. 2.

6. Ibid., p. 6.

7. Nicholas Wolterstorff, *Lament for a Son* (Grand Rapids, Mich.: Eerdmans, 1987), p. 9.

8. Ibid., p. 12.

9. Ibid., p. 77.

10. Ibid., p. 98.

11. Ibid., p.107.

12. Herbert Lockyer, *Psalms: A Devotional Commentary* (Grand Rapids, Mich.: Kregel, 1993), p. 668.

13. William Edgar, "Maximal Minimalism" from *Books & Culture* (Sept/Oct. 1999), www.booksandculture.com/articles/1999/sepoct/9b5014.html.

14. Walter Brueggemann, *Message of the Psalms* (Minneapolis: Augsburg, 1984), pp. 104, 106.

15. Eugene H. Peterson, *A Long Obedience in the Same Direction* (Downers Grove, Ill.: InterVarsity, 1980, 2000), pp. 139-40.

16. Jonathan Aitken, *Psalms for People Under Pressure* (London: Continuum, 2004), pp. x-xii.

17. Ibid., p. xvii.

18. Ibid., p. xviii.

19. Ibid.

Chapter 9

1. John Tebelak, quoted in Fort Wayne Civic Theatre Study Guide for *Godspell,* http://fwcivic.org/StudyGuide-Godspell.pdf.

2. Stephen Schwartz, lyrics from "On the Willows," *Godspell.*

3. C. S. Lewis. *Reflections on the Psalms* (New York: Harcourt Brace Jovanovich), p. 136.

4. Eugene Peterson, *Answering God: The Psalms as Tools for Prayer* (New York: HarperCollins, 1989), p. 98.

5. William L. Holladay, *The Psalms Through Three Thousand Years: Prayerbook of a Cloud of Witnesses* (Minneapolis, Augsburg, 1993), pp. 304-05.

6. Ibid., p. 305. Holladay suggests that the enemies are not so much "men of blood" as "men of idols," and that in Psalm 139:21-22 the psalmist is "affirming his own loyalty to Yahweh."

7. Nathaniel Samuel Murrell, "Tuning Hebrew Psalms to Reggae Rythyms: Rastas' Revolutionary Lamentations for Social Change," *Crosscurrents,* www.crosscurrents.org/murrell.htm.

8. Bob Marley, "Redemption Song," *Uprising,* 1980.

9. Murrell, "Tuning Hebrew Psalms to Reggae Rythyms."

10. Eugene Peterson, *The Message of the Psalms* (Minneapolis: Augsburg Fortress, 1985), p. 75.

11. Simon Srebnik, quoted in Karl A. Plank, "By the Waters of a Death Camp: An Intertextual Reading of Psalm 137," Oxford Journals: *Literature & Theology*, Oxford University Press 2008. http://litthe.oxford journals.org/content/22/2/180.extract.

12. Derek Kidner, *Psalms 73-150: A Commentary on Books III-V of the Psalms* (London: InterVarsity Press, 1975) p. 460.

13. You can read the full account of Melissa Harris-Perry's memories and comments at www.thenation.com/blog/ psalm-137.

14. Peterson, *Answering God,* p. 98.

15. Ibid., p. 100.

16. Patrick D. Miller, *The Way of the Lord* (Grand Rapids, Mich.: Eerdmans, 2007), p. 199.

17. Ibid., p. 200.

18. Peterson, *Answering God,* p. 98.

19. Survivor, "Forgiveness After Rape: Faith and Love in Action," *Chimes* February 9, 2007, http://clubs.calvin. edu/chimes/article.php?id=2009.

Chapter 10

1. Letter of Athanasius, Archbishop of Alexandria, to Marcellinus, www.athanasius.com/psalms/aletterm.htm.

2. Ibid.

3. Ivy Agee, a veteran from Gordonsville, Tennessee, who fought on Omaha Beach. www.foxnews.com/story/0,2933,121829,00.html.

4. Quotations from screenplay *Saving Private Ryan* by Robert Rodat, directed by Steven Spielberg, 1998.

5. Rowland E. Prothero, "The Psalms in Human Life," p. 117. www.archive.org/stream/psalmsinhumanlif00 ernluoft/psalmsinhumanlif00ernluoft_djvu.txt.

6. Quoted in "Robert E. Lee's Religious Views" from www.sonofthesouth.net/leefoundation/Lee_Religious_ Views.htm.

7. From the website http://penelope.uchicago.
    edu/Thayer/E/Gazetteer/People/Robert_E_Lee/
    FREREL/3/14*.html. The website includes a photo-
    graph of the title page of Lee's prayer book.

8. Jon Meacham, *Franklin and Winston: An Intimate Portrait
    of an Epic Friendship* (New York, Random House, 2004),
    p. 152.

9. St. Bernard of Clairvaux, "Letter Promoting the Second
    Crusade," from *Crusades-Encylopedia,* www.crusades-
    encyclopedia.com/psbernardcallforcrusade.html.

10. St. Bernard of Clairvaux, "In Praise of the New
    Knighthood," from www.the-orb.net/encyclop/religion/
    monastic/bernard.html.

11. Matt Rothschild, quoted in www.democracy now.
    org/2005/1/25/the_hidden_passages_in_bushs_inaugural.

12. Mark Noll, *A History of Christianity in the United States
    and Canada* (Grand Rapids, Mich.: Eerdmans, 1992),
    p. 322.

13. Ibid., p. 321.

14. James Luther Mays, *Psalms: A Bible Commentary for
    Teaching and Preaching* (Louisville: John Knox Press,
    1989), p. 436. Psalm 144 is an example of the practice
    of using existing psalms to compose revamped prayers,
    combining earlier material for new compositions
    that fit new realities. For more on this practice see
    chapter 12.

15. "Singing More Psalms in Worship," http://worship.
    calvin.edu/resources/resource-library/singing-
    more-psalms-in-worship.

Chapter 11

1. John Calvin, from his Preface to the Genevan Psalter.
2. William Holladay, *The Psalms through Three Thousand Years: Prayerbook of a Cloud of Witnesses* (Minn.: Augsburg Fortress, 1993), p. 89.
3. Accounts of this discovery are conflicting and varied. This version is a composite based on two sources: William Holladay, *The Psalms through Three Thousand Years*, p. 98, and John C. Trever, *The Dead Sea Scrolls: A Personal Account* (Piscataway, NJ: Gorgias Press, 2003), p. 218.
4. Holladay, *The Psalms through Three Thousand Years*, p. 99.
5. Ibid., pp. 100-03.
6. Ibid., p. 88.
7. Ibid., p. 89.
8. "Athanasius: Five-time Exile for Fighting 'Orthodoxy'"; www.christianitytoday.com/ch/131christians/ theologians/athanasius.html.
9. Letter of Athanasius, Archbishop of Alexandria, to Marcellinus, www.athanasius.com/psalms/aletterm.htm.
10. The translation is taken from *Dead Sea Scrolls Electronic Library*, revised edition (Leiden: Brill, 2006).
11. *Touched by an Angel*, Season 5, www.touched.com/ episodeguide/seasonfive/508.html.
12. Excerpt of "Hymn 9" from William Holladay, *The Psalms through Three Thousand Years*, p. 107. Includes Holladay's notes referencing the texts of biblical psalms.
13. Ibid., p. 108.
14. To hear some of Vos's psalm tunes, visit http://worshipanew.net and click on "The Psalm Project."

15. From author's personal interview with Ken Medema, April 2011.

16. A YouTube recording of "The Tree Song" is available online. At a similar gathering in the 1990s Medema took the theme "Bound for Greater Things" and wrote a song that begins with the first few measures of the Genevan Psalter's version of Psalm 42 and then launches into his own original work. One of his most treasured memories is standing near his grandfather in a church pew as he sang Psalm 42 from the Genevan Psalter with overflowing passion and unending enthusiasm. Years after that convention, whenever Ken sang "Bound for Greater Things" in settings where people knew the Genevan tunes, he would introduce the song by telling the story of his grandpa.

17. *Psalms for All Seasons,* www.faithaliveresources.org.

18. From Medema's song "All My Life" based on Psalm 73.

Epilogue

1. Thomas Merton, *Praying the Psalms* (Collegeville, Minn.: The Liturgical Press, 1956), p. 18.

2. Martin Luther, from his 1528 Preface to the Psalms, quoted in John Dillenberger, ed., *Martin Luther: Selections from His Writings* (New York: Anchor, 1958).

3. Much of this originally appeared in an article previously published online under Kevin Adams, "Ancient Words in a New Light," www.faithandleadership.duke.edu/content/ancient-words-new-light.

4. Not their real names.

Acknowledgments

1. Martin Luther, quoted in John D. Witvliet, *The Biblical Psalms in Christian Worship* (Grand Rapids, Mich.: Eerdmans, 2007), p. 37.